SANDY KOUFAX

As a high school basketball player, caring little for baseball, Sandy Koufax grew up in Brooklyn, which still clasps him to its heart. Today he is the big league pitcher leading the world in strikeouts—and Los Angeles' pride and joy.

Here is the heart-stirring story—with all the statistics—of a great American athlete, already spoken of as the outstanding pitcher of his time.

Author Jerry Mitchell, who also wrote the Grosset Sports Library's hilarious book, THE AMAZING METS, says that mothers across America, daydreaming about this handsome and eligible young bachelor, think what a beautiful catch he would make for a daughter: "My son-in-law, the baseball pitcher. . . ."

GROSSET SPORTS LIBRARY

THE AMAZING METS
By Jerry Mitchell
THE AMERICAN LEAGUE
Ed Fitzgerald, editor
THE ARTFUL DODGERS
By Tom Meany and others
BABE RUTH
By Tom Meany
BASEBALL COMPLETE
By Russ Hodges
BASEBALL'S GREATEST PLAYERS
By Tom Meany
BASEBALL'S HALL OF FAME
By Ken Smith
INSIDE BASEBALL
By Arthur Daley
THE JACKIE ROBINSON STORY
By Arthur Mann
LUCKY TO BE A YANKEE
By Joe DiMaggio
THE MAGNIFICENT YANKEES
By Tom Meany
THE MAKING OF A PRO QUARTERBACK
By Ed Richter
MY GREATEST DAY IN BASEBALL
as told to John P. Carmichael
THE NATIONAL LEAGUE
Ed Fitzgerald, editor
SANDY KOUFAX
By Jerry Mitchell
WILLIE MAYS
By Arnold Hano
WILT CHAMBERLAIN
By George Sullivan
YOGI BERRA
By Joe Trimble

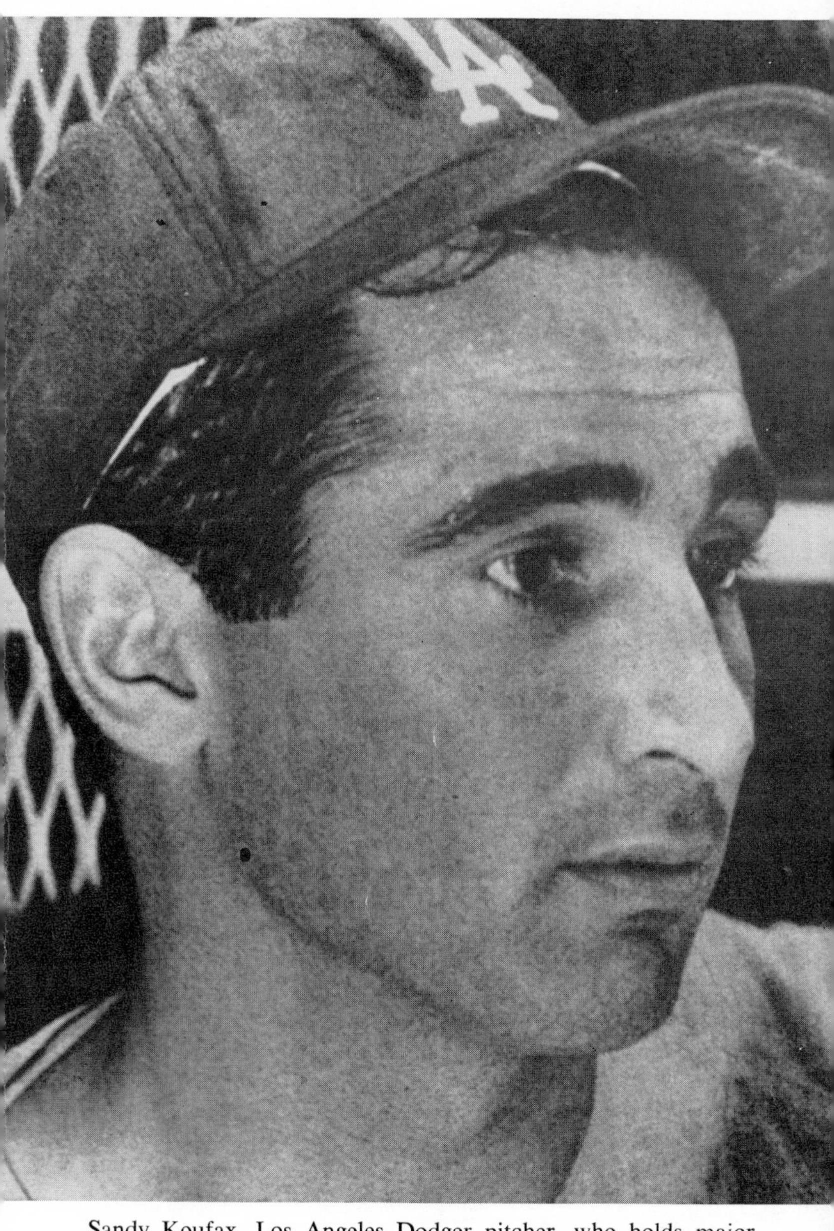

Sandy Koufax, Los Angeles Dodger pitcher, who holds major league baseball's records for the most strikeouts and no-hitters.

Koufax fires the third strike past a Chicago Cub during his fourth no-hitter, a feat achieved by no other major league pitcher.

Pitcher Sandy Koufax and catcher John Roseboro after beating the Yankees 2–1 to take the 1963 World Series in four straight games.

Koufax strokes a clean single to center field, driving in a run. He then pitched four-hit ball to shut out Minnesota 7–0.

Sandy Koufax

By JERRY MITCHELL

GROSSET & DUNLAP
PUBLISHERS • NEW YORK

PUBLISHED SIMULTANEOUSLY IN CANADA
LIBRARY OF CONGRESS CARD CATALOG NUMBER 66–14281

SECOND PRINTING

PHOTOGRAPHS REPRINTED WITH THE
PERMISSION OF WIDE WORLD PHOTOS

PRINTED IN THE UNITED STATES OF AMERICA

To MARGARET

QUOTE-UNQUOTE

"The size of the ball park means nothing to Koufax. He could pitch shutouts in a telephone booth." *Hank Bauer, manager, Baltimore Orioles*

"Koufax is the kind of pitcher who could drive a batter to drink." *Ron Santo, third baseman, Chicago Cubs*

"Hitting against Koufax is like mining hard coal with a toothpick." *Joe Garagiola*

"Umpires often can't see where Koufax's pitches go so they have to judge from the sound of them hitting the catcher's glove. He's very tough for umpires who are hard of hearing." *Casey Stengel*

"Koufax is the greatest Jewish athlete since Samson." *Milton Berle*

"He's one guy who has it licked. The only one else who came close to perfection was Ted Williams.

He had everything wrapped up, the pitchers in one pocket and the umpires in the other." *Gene Mauch, manager, Philadelphia Phillies*

"Koufax is so good he could beat a team made up of the nine best players in the history of baseball." *Paul Richards, former general manager, Houston Colt 45's*

"He has so much speed they ought to handicap him like a horse." *Joe E. Lewis, comedian and horse-player*

"Sandy belongs in another league all by himself." *Wally Moon, outfielder and former Dodger team-mate*

"I was in the bullpen when he pitched his perfect game against the Cubs. That's about as close as I want to be when he's throwing." *Ed Bailey, catcher, Chicago Cubs*

"I expect him to pitch a no-hit, no-run game every time he starts. I'm only surprised when somebody gets a hit off him." *Don Drysdale, pitcher, Los Angeles Dodgers*

"He has such style that he's the only pitcher I'd pay my way into the park just to watch him warmup." *Sam Mele, manager, Minnesota Twins*

"Gosh, now that the Dodgers have found that Koufax can pitch with only two days' rest, all of us are finished." *Chub Feeney, general manager, San Francisco Giants*

"Koufax is the greatest pitcher alive. And maybe dead. The only thing I can do better than Sandy is sing and dance." *Mudcat Jim Grant, pitcher, Minnesota Twins*

"Koufax pitched like a man who was auditioning for Mamie Van Doren . . . The way the Yankees hit against Koufax–if they had shown the same attacking capabilities during the Civil War–Orval Faubus might be president today." *Jackie Gleason*

INTRODUCTION

As A BOY of sixteen, Sandy Koufax was good at just about any sport he tried. If he ever imagined himself a great basketball player, he never thought of himself as a baseball star. He didn't really care much about baseball, but when the basketball season ended, he naturally gravitated to sandlot baseball. No one in Brooklyn could possibly have imagined that this quiet, shy kid would someday be called the greatest pitcher of all time.

Although Sandy went to college on a basketball scholarship, he pitched his way onto the varsity baseball team his first year, and before long the major league scouts were looking him over.

At a tryout for the New York Giants, most of his pitches were too wild for the catcher to stop without a net. They promptly forgot about him.

Later, a retired pitcher who scouted for the Boston Red Sox in the New York metropolitan area, asked Charley Sheerin, who had been the boy's high school baseball coach, to arrange a private workout so that he could pass judgement. The scout watched, shook his head and said: "He'll never make a pitcher. Never."

At nineteen, when he was a bonus baby in the spring training camp of the Brooklyn Dodgers, a kindly coach shooed him off to one of the less public practice fields so that he wouldn't be embarrassed before strangers when errant throws went high over the catcher's head.

It took a long, long time—even after he became a Dodger.

In his first six seasons with the Dodgers he won a total of only thirty-six games and his earned-run average in one of them rose to an inelegant 4.88. Wildness was his constant companion. In 1960 he was so discouraged that many thought he would turn in his uniform and forget about baseball.

The truth is that Sandy Koufax was the kid who almost didn't make it. He was plagued with self doubt before every game. Now it was getting to him every time he threw the ball—worrying that if he didn't make the pitch count for a strike he might not get to pitch again for three or four weeks; worrying that if he walked the batter he might be yanked out of the game; worrying what manager Walter Alston might be thinking; worrying about the guy warming up in the bullpen. And the more he worried the harder he burned them in—and the oftener his pitch was the wrong pitch or went completely wide of the mark.

The spring of 1961 found Sandy on a plane bound for a B-squad game at Orlando. Sitting next to him was his old buddy, catcher Norm Sherry.

"Look, Koo," mused Sherry, breaking into Sandy's

thoughts, "why don't you try easying up on your fast ball and stop trying to blast 'em by the batters? You throw less hard, you've still got one of the best fast balls in the league, but you'll be throwing more accurately. You'll put it where it wants to go. You ought to try more curve balls and change-ups."

Sandy's answer is in the record books. That season he won eighteen games. He struck out 269 batters to break Christy Mathewson's record of 267. The pitcher who had wondered if he was in the right trade was finally on his way. Sherry's suggestion had also changed Sandy's point of view: "Now I'm excited about playing baseball," he said.

Still a shy guy, the public has thought Koufax aloof. He insists this isn't true. "I'm normal, that's all." And normal he is all right, as normal as any clean-cut American youth can be who drives a long fast car with a gorgeous Hollywood starlet type on the seat beside him, as normal as anyone whose annual take-home pay is in the high five figures, whose home is a romantic bachelor hideaway in the San Fernando Valley with a two-car garage and just a small secluded swimming pool in the back yard, and whose looks and voice qualify him for a movie lead any time he wants it.

The boy grew older. In 1965, a mature twenty-nine, Koufax won twenty-eight times for the National League pennant-winning Los Angeles Dodgers. Included in the big bundle was a perfect game—twenty-seven men up, twenty-seven men down and no return checks. He became the eighth man in modern baseball history to work a faultless game and the first ever to pitch four no-hitters.

He hummed past Bob Feller's major league record of 348 strikeouts in one season, hiking it to 382. He led the National League pitchers with the lowest earned-run average for the fourth season in succession. Then he won two games in shutout style in the 1965 World Series with the Minnesota Twins, dominating that classic as no pitcher had before.

Sandy had kept himself in haircut money with a $70,000 contract for the 1965 season, plus a $500 bonus for his no-hitter.

After banking his winning World Series share, a cool $10,297.43, he locked up his house and went on a well-earned Hawaiian holiday. Talk about a new $100,000 Dodger contract could wait. So could the pleasant task of picking up a new Corvette compliments of *Sport* magazine. It was the second time in three years he had been voted the car as the outstanding performer of the World Series. His two-car garage was coming in handy.

SANDY KOUFAX

CHAPTER ONE

A LOT OF exciting baseball history would never have been written had young Koufax concentrated on a basketball career in his Brooklyn post-high school days.

It could have happened. He was called a basketball player of tremendous potential. The player-hungry New York Knickerbockers of the National Basketball Association, always on the lookout for local material that would mean longer lines at the box office, held a scrimmage against the Lafayette team in the high school gymnasium early in 1953.

Sandy lined up against Harry Gallatin, the Knicks' ace rebounder. He dunked a few and out jumped Gallatin a number of times. When it was over Gallatin and teammate Dick McGuire congratulated the boy on an exceptional performance.

"I wouldn't be surprised if we come back for that kid one of these days," Gallatin told Frank Rabinowitz, the Lafayette coach.

"He has a real future in pro basketball," the Knicks' player went on. "He could easily develop into one of the good ones. He's big and strong and when he grabs the ball it stays his. He's got a tremendous leap and for such a big kid, he moves like a cat. With him I'd say it's just a question of time and experience."

Later, Rabinowitz said, "You just knew he'd get better and better in basketball. He could dribble with either hand as well as any kid I've ever seen and his big hands gave him remarkable control of the ball. And he had great motor ability."

Harry Ostro, the Lafayette football coach, wanted the big youngster on his squad. He had visions of Sandy smacking the enemy lines as a backfield man or tackle.

"You could see he had great possibilities," said the coach. "He could throw a football almost the length of a football field like it was out of a seige gun. I thought he'd make a fine player and tried to get him to go out for the team seriously.

"Sandy preferred to play basketball, however, and the football and basketball seasons conflicted. I remember thinking at the time he had no real desire to be an athlete. How wrong I was. Sandy had it all the time in his own quiet way."

The youngster's only athletic activity at Lafayette High, aside from basketball, was baseball, but not until his senior year.

"In our baseball program we had a tryout day for the pitchers one day and another the next day for the outfielders and another on the third day for the infielders.

"He came out with the infield candidates. He was tall and rangy and I made him our first baseman. He could field all right but he couldn't hit worth a hoot. Well, maybe he hit something like .200 for us.

"Then one afternoon we were playing Brooklyn Tech. Sandy came up with two men on base. A home run would have won the game for us, 4–3 but he hit one about fifteen feet from the fence and we lost it, 3–1."

Sheerin had a professional eye, having played the outfield for the Philadelphia Phillies in 1936. He had batted .264 and faced Dizzy Dean five times that season, getting three hits. Another time he knocked Carl Hubbell, the great screwball pitcher of the New York Giants, out of the box with a double against the fence.

Sheerin says he may never live down the fact that he had Sandy on his team and didn't use him as a pitcher.

"I'm reminded of it," he says, "time and again. Sandy is the greatest pitcher who ever lived. His record proves that."

Sanford Koufax, the son of Evelyn and Irving Koufax, was born in Brooklyn on December 30, 1935. There was no athletic background in the family. His father, a Manhattan attorney, took his sports strictly as a spectator.

Around his Brooklyn neighborhood, Sandy was known as a boy basketball whiz who played baseball just for want of something to do in the summer and because most of his friends played the game.

Basketball was his first love. He played three-man basketball when they couldn't get two full teams together in the school yards and playgrounds. If no kids were around he would practice shooting basketballs by the hour. As a boy's camp counselor at Catskill Mountain resorts, he played even more basketball with the other camp aides and the kids.

He remembers playing some catch-as-can baseball

on a school field near his home. He was about eleven years old. "None of the kids ever seemed to want to be the catcher," he recalls. "You know how it is with kids. If you happen to have a good pitcher the only other real ball player on the lot is the catcher. The others just stand around and yell. I guess I wanted to be in the action as much as possible–like in basketball–so I volunteered to be catcher."

There was an equipment problem. The catcher's glove wasn't made for a left-hander. Young Koufax solved the problem by taking a right-handed catcher's glove, yanking it inside out, stuffing it with straw and having the shoemaker down the block stitch on a strap.

Then the Koufax family–Sandy, his mother, father and older sister–moved to Rockville Center, Long Island. After four years, however, they moved back to Brooklyn. (In 1958, when Walter O'Malley, whose roots also were in Brooklyn, packed up the Dodgers and headed the California gold rush, the family moved again, this time to Los Angeles.)

In Rockville Center there was no handy school athletic field. "It was hard trying to find a place to play ball," Sandy said. "And it wasn't much fun playing ball on the streets where you had no real space and you always had to watch out for cars. It was a lot easier going to a school yard and playing basketball. No matter how small the school you always found there were a few baskets in the yard."

About this time a Brooklyn man named Secol whom the kids called "Pop" founded what soon began to be called "The Ice Cream League." Most of the games were played on the Parade Grounds, a famous old field in Flushing that contained about ten baseball diamonds as well as playground facilities and was crowded with athletes, junior grade, every day.

Kids from about fourteen years of age up formed the teams in the Ice Cream League. Koufax became a member of the Tomahawks, a team from his own Bensonhurst section. Years later he can still rattle off the names of that early outfit:

"Hal Laufer, Jay Lichtman, Howard Pasternack, Stanley Lawrence and Dave Applebaum were the outfielders. Emil Quadrino, Stanley Seigel, Joe Siegel, Larry Elorich and Ted Hausner were the infielders. Lenny Gross was the catcher. The pitchers were Mike Field and me. Mike was a right-hander, our big pitcher. I was the other one, the left-hander."

"Sandy lived in an apartment house on Seventeenth Avenue off the Shore Road then," Hal Laufer recalls. "We'd usually meet at somebody's house in Bensonhurst and one of the parents drive us to the Parade Grounds.

"We had a big deal series in 1952 with the Scorpions for the championship of the Ice Cream League. We won it, three games to one, with Mike Field winning two games and Koufax one. By golly but Sandy was wild. He'd either walk them or strike them out—he was something."

"I remember him well," says Milt Gold, director of the Jewish Community House of Bensonhurst. "He was a gawky kid at first but grew fast and big. A quiet kid but good in almost evrey one of our sports activity—swimming, wrestling, basketball—everything."

One spring day Milt Laurie, a friend who had noticed the effortless manner in which Koufax fired the ball across the infield as the Lafayette High School first baseman, suggested that Sandy give baseball a serious try as a pitcher. Laurie, a long-time Brooklyn sandlot figure, managed the Parkviews. They competed against the Cadets and Nathan's Famous, sponsored by the Coney Island hot dog foundry.

"You could see that he had that wonderful arm," says Laurie. "You'd have had to be blind not to. Honestly, even then he threw the ball as hard as any pitcher I'd ever seen. And he was still growing bigger and stronger.

"With a live arm like that you could make quite a pitcher, I told him. Sandy said he thought he'd do as a basketball player but he'd give pitching a try. We worked on it. He was as wild as anything, never knew where the ball was going when he went all out with a pitch but what he threw really jumped. It was no contest against kids his age, or for that matter older ones. They only *thought* they saw the ball."

But basketball still claimed him. After he was named an All-City forward by the schoolboy basketball writers of the metropolitan district, the offers of college basketball scholarships poured in. He could have gone to any of the top colleges on the Pacific Coast, any of the Big Ten or any of the Eastern basket biggies. After careful deliberation he chose the University of Cincinnati.

"At the time I was giving some thought to eventually becoming an architect," he says, "and Cincinnati had one of the leading schools of architecture in the country."

Koufax played on the freshman basketball team at Cincinnati. In those days freshmen were allowed to play varsity baseball. The frosh basketball coach was also in charge of varsity baseball, so when the court season ended Sandy told him that he had played some high school baseball and would like to try out for the ball club.

"By then I knew darn well I couldn't hit worth a lick," he says. "So I did what a lot of other fellows do when they discover the same thing—pitch. I knew that at least I could throw the ball hard. I figured I had nothing to lose and I'd keep active in sports."

Freshman Koufax won his first two games for the Bearcats' varsity, beating Wayne University and the University of Louisville. He won three and lost one for the season, striking out fifty-one men in thirty-two innings. He walked thirty and yielded sixteen hits and ten earned runs.

The major league scouts? They had of course come running after Sandy struck out seventeen in his first varsity start. He had immediately become a youngster they wanted to see more of.

He pitched some more sandlot ball when he went home for the summer. Scouts covering the area for the New York Yankees, Pittsburgh Pirates, Boston Red Sox, Philadelphia Phillies, Cleveland Indians Milwaukee Braves, Detroit Tigers, Chicago Cubs, New York Giants and others boosted the attendance at the Parkviews' games.

The Giants' scout invited him to the Polo Grounds for a tryout. He reported with a dozen other prospects who had been followed as they played for various New York and New Jersey teams.

"My first tryout was something," he says. "I was scared to death even though there weren't any people in the stands and all the others, except for some second string players on the Giants who were helping out or getting in some practice, were as young as I."

Frank Shellenback, the old pitcher working for the Giants as a scout and talent inspector, watched from the sidelines. Bobby Hoffman was his catcher. Sandy hit the screen behind Hoffman as often as he hit his glove. "I was glad to get out of there." Sandy recalls only too vividly. "I never heard from the Giants again."

In talking to major league clubs the young man stressed his need for a bonus payment. Not a big fat one—though many clubs were in the habit then of shelling out fantastic sums to unproven kids—but a bonus.

"After all," he says, "signing with a major league club meant that I would have to leave Cinncincinnati—giving up my basketball scholarship in order to play baseball. It meant I would need money in case I decided to return to college at the end of every season."

At the time a big, pleasant man named Jimmy Murphy was writing a schoolboy sports column for the New York *World Telegram and Sun.* Jimmy had an intense interest in kids and high school sports. He was an old semi-pro pitcher, a reformed spitball pitcher, and if there was anything he knew all about it was pitching.

Murphy spotted this wild, hard-throwing young left-hander pitching for the Parkviews of the Coney Island League against the Cadets and immediately liked what he saw. It wasn't just that the Cadets were so baffled by the fast balls and crackling curve that Koufax threw. It was something else.

"The kid was throwing a 'bloodball' most of the game," says Murphy admiringly. "He had a bad blood blister on his pitching hand and when it broke midway through the game, there was blood all over the ball he threw. I was impressed with his moxie. He just wiped off his fingers and kept on pitching. I'd never seen anything like it."

Murphy was also a dedicated Dodger fan. He dated back to their glory days, when Uncle Wilbert Robinson was manager and their cast of characters included Casey Stengel, Zack Wheat, Moon Miller, Jake Daubert, Ivy Olson, Jeff Pfeffer and others celebrated in early Brooklyn song and story.

Uncle Robbie liked big, strong pitchers, particularly if they were what he called "pleasingly wild." From the moment he saw young Koufax throw his errant fireball, Jimmy thought that here was a pitcher Robbie would have loved.

He thought surely he saw in Sandy the makings of another Dazzy Vance, Jumbo Jim Elliott, Doug McWeeney, Al Mamaux, Guy Cantrell, Pfeffer—one of the shot-putting stars of the Dodger past. He got in touch with Brooklyn officials and suggested that they look the young left-hander over before it was too late.

Al Campanis, the chief Dodger scout in the home district, watched Koufax pitch soon thereafter and was as impressed as Murphy. "I actually had trouble seeing the ball at times," says Al, "he was that fast. Here was one we couldn't afford to miss so I set up a tryout date at Ebbets Field."

"I'd been there as a fan occasionally," recalls Sandy. "In fact I can remember my father taking me to Ebbets Field for the first time way back in 1947 when they had those great teams. When Pete Reiser was the Dodger centerfielder, a terrific runner and one of the best hitters in the business.

"The Dodgers were losing a 1-0 game to the Phillies that afternoon but they managed to put on a great rally in the late innings, finally winning it. I remember Reiser hitting the ball between two of the outfielders and flying around the bases for an inside the park home run. I talked about that run for days."

His Dodger tryout came in September of 1954 before a night game. He wasn't as nervous as he had been the day the Giants had looked him over at the Polo Grounds. Rube Walker was the catcher. Manager Walter Alston, Al Campanis, scout Andy High and others watched. They liked what they saw. Afterwards, Buzzy Bavasi, the general manager, sat down with Sandy and his father. The club offered a $14,000 bonus, plus $6,000, the minimum first year salary. An appointment was made for the actual contract signing at the club's downtown office. Sandy didn't show up.

"He came in a few days later," recalls a Brooklyn official. "It seems he had been in Pittsburgh working out with the Pirates, who were very strong on him. He told us that other clubs were offering him more money but that he was going to stick with us. He could easily have gone to another club. There was nothing on paper binding him to the Brooklyn club. But he kept his word. A class guy, even then."

"We gave the matter a lot of thought at home," says Koufax. "We weighed all the possibilities. I finally decided that if I was going to make it as a big leaguer I would make it best, everything considered, in Brooklyn. Besides I liked the way the Dodgers treated me. They were a friendly bunch from Bavasi and Campanis down to the players I'd met the day I worked out at Ebbets Field."

Koufax had talked to representatives of many clubs in both leagues. Pittsburgh interested him the most at first because he felt he might have a better chance of making the Pirates—then a confirmed second division club—than the veteran-stocked first division Dodgers. Jimmy Murphy recalls that he had seen Joe LaBate, the Phillies' scout in the Brooklyn-Long Island area, talking to the boy one day at a sandlot game.

Someone asked Sandy if the knowledge that major league eyes were in the audience bothered him.

"Not much. Maybe I was getting a little used to that sort of attention by then. I knew the Phillies were going to hold a big tryout in Long Island City. I had a good day but I never heard from them. Anyway, that didn't bother me too much because there were other offers."

By next summer, someone said, he'd probably be pitching aganist the best players in baseball.

"Funny but I never thought of it as being that close," Sandy said, "but maybe I'd better start. The closest I'd been to Stan Musial was in the hotel elevator the day I was in Pittsburgh for a tryout. The Cardinals were playing the Pirates that day. It never occurred to me I might be pitching against him real soon."

He was a nineteen-year-old bonus baby when he reported to the Dodgers training camp in Vero Beach, Florida, in March of 1955. Under the bonus rule then in existence, they had to keep him on their roster for two years and couldn't farm him out to one of their minor league clubs where he could get much needed experience.

Sandy was scared and anxious. He had gone to Columbia University during the winter and maybe he wished he was still an architecture student there with nothing to worry about except the next exam. He wasn't the only one. The major league training grounds in Florida, Arizona and elsewhere, were plentifully sprinkled that spring with fuzz-cheeked youths who had been wooed by bonus payments. Like the others he must have thought about the reactions of the many veterans who hadn't received fat sums for signing. Here he was, taking up a spot on the roster that might have been occupied by an experienced player who might help the club win the pennant or a position that would mean more money.

Here he was, the rawest of rookies surrounded by established stars—by aging veterans trying to hold onto their jobs. At the most he had been in twenty-five ball games—college and sandlot—and not one of them for money. Everyone in his Brooklyn neighborhood had been surprised when he turned out to be a sought-after strikeout artist. All of them were pleased and rooting for the kid down the block to make good. But they were rooting back in Brooklyn, many, many miles from Vero Beach.

CHAPTER TWO

DODGERTOWN WAS A sprawling place inland from Vero Beach. It had been converted into a baseball training camp from a naval air station years before by Branch Rickey, when he had been president of the Dodgers. It was an impressive sight to a raw recruit from the streets of Brooklyn.

There was an administration building that included a large cafeteria-style dining room, hospital facilities, recreation rooms, club offices, a lounging lobby and a small store that sold sodas, candy, cigarettes, postcards and comic books. It also served as a post office. Around the administration building were converted barracks where the players lived two to a room, and one that was used as a movie house.

Koufax, that first day in camp, lined up to fill out a registration card and undergo a physical examination. He went to the supply room, signing for two hand towels, one bath towel, two sheets, a pillow case and two blankets. (Nights in Vero Beach could be cold to the surprise of northern boys.) On top of that went his baseball equipment—pants, shirt, belt, stockings, cap, and windbreaker—also signed for. His spiked shoes, undershirt, sweatshirt, and shorts he provided himself.

Sandy found himself paired with another rookie. Both were fortunate in that they were assigned a room in a wing of the administration building. Instead of the bunks provided in the barracks, they were the sturdy metal cots once used by Navy Air Officers. Between two closets cut into the cardboard thin walls hung a faded print: "Sunset on the Ohio." A washbasin stood in one corner and a small writing table in the other.

On the daily rule sheet handed all the players, Sandy read:

7:00 All personnel will be called.
7:30 Breakfast will be served in the cafeteria until 8:45.
9:00 Calisthenics on the assembly grounds near Diamond No. One, under the direction of Al Campanis.
9:30 Report to the Diamond, or Instructors you have been assigned to.
12:00 Luncheon will be served until 1:45 p.m.
5:30 Dinner. Cafeteria doors will be closed at 7:00.
11:00 All lights out. All players will be in their rooms.

The sheet contained other rules, warnings and general information. Sandy read on:

Conserve food. Eat enough but don't over indulge. Remember, you are in training.
No smoking in cafeteria or lecture halls.

No drinking intoxicants in any form whatsoever.
No gambling.
No horse play, particularly in shower rooms. Serious injury might result.
Baseball shoes must be removed before entering all buildings.
No player is to leave the field without consulting the manager.
Vero Beach is OFF-LIMITS because of the dangerous surf at times. If you must swim use the pool adjacent to the shuffleboard court.
If you are ill report to our physician in Room 19, Headquarters.
Help yourself to the free orange juice in the big barrel in front of the Administration Building.
Don't bother the cooks or kitchen help for between meal snacks.
It will pay you to hustle here.

His first morning in the clubhouse was something to remember. He entered gingerly. Before their lockers in the big room were the Dodger greats—Pee Wee Reese, Gil Hodges, Roy Campanella, Don Newcombe, Carl Furillo, Carl Erskine, Clem Labine, Preacher Roe, Joe Black, Jackie Robinson and Johnny Podres. And Rube Walker, Sandy's battery-mate at his Ebbets Field tryout, Gino Cimoli, Irv Palica, Chico Fernandez, Charley Neal, George Shuba, Billy Loes, Don Hoak and Jim (Junior) Gilliam.

Babe Hamburger saw Sandy's bewildered look and took him in tow. Hamburger, a stout, friendly fellow, who had started in the Brooklyn organization in the late 1920's as a clubhouse boy and mender of uniforms on a sewing machine in the annex, was the Dodgers' general handyman. He served as guide, baggage controller, father confessor to the youngsters, announcer at Dodgertown ball games, assistant secretary, and bartender in the press lounge.

Walter Alston, the manager, came in shortly, walked to the center of the clubhouse and said, "Some of you are new here. So don't hesitate to ask the coaches or the older players for help. Don't think you know it all.

"Do what you're told on the field and do it the best you can. Keep your eyes and ears open. Keep moving. Don't leave any field without permission. Now let's go!"

At the end of that long first day, Sandy walked wearily back to his quarters, remembering to take off his spiked shoes at the door. The shower felt extra fine. Then he sat down and wrote his first letter home. It felt good to hit the sack that night. A few days later the aches really caught up with him as they did, sooner or later, with all the players—stars, free agents hopeful of being assigned to one of the club's better farm teams, and raw rookies like himself.

The fourth day in camp found Sandy at the head of the line when Phil Rosa, the bespectacled little postmaster of Dodgertown, opened his window to deal out the afternoon mail.

"Okay boys," said Rosa. "Let's go. Name?"

"Koufax. Sandy Koufax."

"Koufax," Rosa said, then looked at the postmarks of the two letters.

"From Brooklyn, eh? You sure came to the right camp. I hope a hometown boy makes good. Say, you any relation to the Irving Koufaxes? They used to live near me."

"That's my father," said Sandy.

"Now I remember you," said Rosa. "You used to be always fooling around with a basketball with the neighborhood kids. I remember they used to say you were going to be a professional basketball player some day. Well, nice handwriting your father has here . . ."

Sandy was still boyish enough to be a little overawed by one of his dad's accomplishments and pleased at Rosa's interest.

"You should see him write," he said with a grin. "He's ambidextrous. He'll take a pencil and write right-handed, then write just the same left-handed. Then he writes backwards with the left hand and forwards with the right at the same time. Darnest thing you ever saw."

Howls were beginning to come from the other players in line.

"Hey Koufax," one impatient pitcher toward the rear yelled, "break it up. Get your mail and scram. What is this anyway, a family reunion?"

Soon Koufax became known as a pitcher who, when he wasn't doing unorthodox things on the field, did them off it.

He was frequently seen reading books, when the others in the lobby chairs or recreation rooms were absorbed in comics or murder mystery magazines. He was sometimes seen wandering around the new housing development between Dodgertown and downtown Vero Beach, studying the many new ranch type and split-level houses with a professional eye. It was the architectural student in him.

One morning in the pitcher's box, taking his turn at fielding balls and throwing to second base to rub out an imaginary runner, Sandy wheeled around counterclockwise—the wrong way for a left-handed pitcher. Coach Jake Pitler blinked, then told Preacher Roe, one of the older pitchers, to take the kid aside and straighten him out.

But Sandy said he wasn't that green, honest. It was just that his arm was a bit stiff and he didn't want to tax it by going through the full wheeling motion. To save effort he spun the other way and just flipped the ball to second.

He was as wild as advertised. Once a spectator, when Koufax was making the catcher jump around for pitches, was heard saying: "Why he throws like a girl."

Joe Becker, a tall, lean man out of St. Louis, was the coach in direct charge of the Dodgers' many pitchers. A former catcher, he had been up and down and all around the baseball map, working for the St. Louis Cardinals, Cleveland Indians and New York Giants. When he managed the Toronto club of the International League, Becker often clashed with Walter Alston, then running Brooklyn's Montreal farm club in the same league. Alston noticed that the weakest Toronto teams always seemed to have strong pitching. So when pitching coach Ted Lyons left the Brooklyn organization, Alston asked Becker to fill the vacancy.

It soon proved to be one of Alston's shrewdest moves. Becker did much to help the Brooklyn pitchers Johnny Podres and Don Drysdale, and particularly the younger ones, Koufax and Billy Loes—the highest priced Dodger bonus baby, who got $21,000 and an automobile from Branch Rickey in 1949.

They didn't come to camp any greener than Koufax. He exhibited little co-ordination on the mound and knew nothing about the art of pitching. Pee Wee Reese, then the Brooklyn shortstop, says that when he saw first Sandy in the Vero Beach camp he told himself the boy would never make a pitcher.

Becker, watching the youngster in early days of that first spring, decided it would be easier on Koufax if he did his pitching on one of the more remote diamonds, rather than one of those where the townspeople and tourists flocked to watch the Dodgers every morning and afternoon. The pitching coach also decided that Koufax should spend a lot of time in what was known as the "string area" in the Dodgers' baseball foundry.

The "strings" were a vestigal reminder of the days of Rickey, founder of the Vero Beach sweaty assembly line. A framework of wooden gibbets like soccer goalposts were strung with cords, outlining a vertical rectangle representing the strike zone between a man's knees and shoulders.

Becker would often stroll over from one of the main diamonds to the string area, hidden from the sightseer behind one of the barracks, to watch Koufax and the others who had difficulty throwing the ball anywhere near the strike zone.

Koufax was often nervous then and worked hurriedly. Now and then Becker, standing behind him, would say "Toe in, now. That's right, toe in. And take it easy. You're going like a race horse."

When the kid got the range, his pitches whistled through the lower corners to the waiting catcher, but every now and then the ball would get away from him. Wild pitches sailed over the catcher's head and smacked high against the canvas backstop.

"Oh nuts!" Sandy would say.

"That's all right," Becker would counter. "Just take it easy."

Joe Black, the relief pitcher had been the National League rookie-of-the-year in 1952, winning fifteen games while losing four, a bust in 1953, an exile to the Montreal farm in 1954, and was now trying to make a 1955 comeback. Black had just finished a turn at pitching to the strings.

"Everybody throws them there," said Joe. "I know a fellow who used to throw them even over the canvas backstop."

"That's right," said Becker. "Pitcher by the name of Bob Feller, wasn't it?"

Black nodded.

The next time he reared back and threw the ball, Koufax winced and grunted. He had pulled a muscle in his side. He began to lob the ball to the catcher as if in pain.

"Don't you throw if it hurts you," said Becker. "Matter of fact that's enough for you today. Don't throw any more. Do some running instead. Take some turns around the outfield and then take your shower."

"Maybe I should throw some more," said Sandy. "Maybe if I just keep throwing easy for a while the soreness will work itself out."

"Why don't you have the trainer, Doc Wendler, rub you down?" said Joe. "He works for you too, you know. Don't be afraid to ask him to. Might turn out to be the smartest thing you've done."

"How about that?" a visiting journalist said to Becker. "Is Black a coach too?"

"No, he's out here throwing to the strings too," said Becker. "But why shouldn't Joe give some advice?

He's pitched enough so he must have plenty of advice to spare. Besides, he's remembering what Alston said the first day about how the kids shouldn't hesitate to go to the older players for help. Joe didn't wait to be asked. There should be more like him around."

Koufax was standing in front of his locker later, tying his tie while listening to the back-country humor of Elwin Charles (Preacher) Roe, the veteran left-hander from Ash Flat, Arkansas.

"If I thought to bring my houn' dog to camp with me, you an' I could get some extra practice pitching to the strings even after the catchers quit for the day," Preacher was saying. "My houn' dog's name is Mr. Bones, on account he's always burying one.

"When I want to throw down home before coming to camp, I just go out on a field with Mr. Bones and a dozen baseballs. I throw to a spot on a backstop an' Mr. Bones waits until I've thrown maybe a half dozen an' then he fetches 'em back to me as fast as anything."

Sandy grinned. One of the pleasures of life at Vero Beach, he had discovered, was listening to the stories of Preacher Roe and Roy Campanella, the stocky, friendly catcher. They helped him forget the often dull and tiresome routine practiced at what sports writers referred to as the Dodger compound.

"They asked me again today if I would fly, same as they did before," the Preacher was saying. "They plan to do a lot of flying in their private plane. The only one of its kind, I think, that hasn't been shot down by a boy with a BB gun. I told them no again.

"If the good Lord had meant Ol' Preach to fly, He'd have given me wings."

There were other laughs around Dodgertown, most

of them supplied by John (The Senator) Griffin, a stout, care-free character who had been the Dodgers' club-house man for many years, and Babe Hamburger, a kindred soul. They ran a never-ending vaudeville act.

The Senator kept a club-house closet full of old-fashioned, knee-length bathing suits, baggy clown pants, masks, and outrageous hats. When the Dodgers went into a slump or there seemed to be some need for laughs, he would get up some outlandish costume.

Campanella told Sandy of the day when the Dodgers were dining on the porch overlooking the swimming pool of the Jaragua Hotel, the spring they trained in the Dominican Republic.

"We're all pitchin' into the chow when suddenly there's the sound of wailing sirens," said Roy. "And into sight comes about a dozen motorcycle cops leadin' a horse-drawn carriage that was decked all over with flowers.

"Mr. Rickey was sittin' at the next table with Buzzy Bavasi. He raised those big, heavy eyebrows of his an' says,

" 'Judas priest!'—Mr. Rickey talked like that—'Judas priest! Who in the world is this celebrity comin' to our hotel?' Nobody answered 'cause nobody knew.

"Well the police climbed out of their motorcycles, drew their guns an' formed a sort of guard of honor lane into the hotel. An' who do you suppose stepped out of the carriage but The Senator an' Babe, both of 'em wearing nothin' but those crazy striped and dotted bathin' suits folks used to wear way back in the 1890's an' both carrying big parasols.

"They walked like the most dignified fellas in the

whole world to the edge of the pool and then fell in an' you shoulda heard us all—even Mr. Rickey—howl. All along I guess most of us suspected Trujillo, the dictator, was puttin' on a big, special welcome for somebody."

A visitor asked Koufax what he thought of the risk of having to stick around with the Dodgers for two seasons before the bonus rule permitted the club to send him to one of their minor league farm clubs like St. Paul or Montreal, or better still one in a lower classification, where he would be able to pitch regularly.

"I've given it a lot of thought," said the soft-spoken youngster. "I gave up that five-year scholarship at the University of Cincinnati to sign with this club, you know. It was quite a decision.

"I don't think sitting on the Dodger bench for two years will be too terrific a handicap. I expect to learn on the bench or sitting in the bullpen. I'll learn listening to the older pitchers and watching them from so close-up.

"I'll probably pitch a little this year, and then maybe, with luck, I'll pitch a whole lot more next year. There's bound to be games so well lost they won't want to use up other pitchers.

"I've made up my mind that I'll give baseball five years. These first two with the Dodgers, then three more, probably in the minors since they'll be able to send me out on option then to a farm club.

"If I'm not back up here with the Dodgers by then, I'll give the whole thing up and become an architect. As it is, I plan to study architecture in New York, probably at Columbia, during the winter."

Sandy was still bothered by a sore back, developed that day he had been pitching to the strings with Joe Black, but was beginning to come around. His fastball was the talk of the camp. So were his wild streaks.

There was a stretch during that first spring when Sandy was so nervous and tense, so worried about making good that he did no pitching to speak of for a week. Then he developed a sore arm. "I tried to throw as hard as I could too much," he says. "But that sore arm taught me something. It taught me that pitching for a professional ball club is a lot different than pitching in college or on the sandlots, where a fellow pitches only once a week. Here I was overdoing it like crazy, throwing as hard as I could day after day."

Between his sore arm and a couple of sprained ankles, Sandy's first spring didn't amount to much. The club finally decided to put him on the disabled list for the first thirty days of the season. The move also enabled the Dodgers to keep another prospect, not in the bonus category, on the roster for further inspection in that time.

It was June 6, 1955 before Walter Alston decided to risk Sandy in a National League game. He pitched two innings of relief ball in a losing game with the Milwaukee Braves allowing one hit, walking one batter, and striking out two others. It wasn't a bad beginning.

Four days later Alston called upon him to do another relief job in a thoroughly lost game, this time against the New York Giants. Sandy pitched one inning, allowed two hits and walked one man.

Something special happened to the nineteen-year-old in Forbes Field, Pittsburgh on July 6. The manager wound him up and started him in a ball game for the first time. His versus was Vernon Law, an established pitcher for the Pirates.

Koufax proceeded to turn in some stout pitching that for a while overcame a grievous lack of control. He handed out bases on balls like a fellow contributing to some needy charity. He walked six men in four innings, a rough handicap, yet the Pirates couldn't get a run across the plate so hard was his fastball.

However, when Sandy walked two more Pirates after two had singled in the fifth inning, forcing one run home, Alston thought it time for some help from the bullpen. He brought in Ed Roebuck, the relief pitcher, who finally lost the game in the late innings.

Sandy's maiden game record showed three hits in four-and-two-thirds innings, four strikeouts and eight bases on balls.

"He had made one hundred and six pitches," the manager explained. "Enough for a normal nine-inning game."

Not until August 27 was Koufax given another opportunity to start a game. This time it was at Crosley Field, Cincinnati, against a strong clubbing collection of Redlegs. This time he showed them something special, pitching a gaudy two-hit shutout to win a tough 1-0 decision. It made good reading for the folks back in Brooklyn the next day.

Ted Kluzewski, the big, muscular Cincinnati first baseman, singled through a hole in the infield to right field in the first inning, but Sandy turned back that threat.

The next Redleg hit didn't come until there were

two out in the ninth. Then outfielder Sam Mele, (as manager of the Minnesota Twins, he watched helplessly as Sandy shut out his American League champions in two games of the World Series ten years later) doubled into the field corner. Sandy took care of this threat by getting Rocky Bridges on a meek pop-up to shortstop Pee Wee Reese.

The Dodgers on the field rushed to pound their boy wonder on the back. Those in the dugout poured out to do more of the same. Even the Cincinnati fans roared their approval.

Upstairs in the radio booth Cincinnati broadcaster Waite Hoyt told his listeners. "We've just seen a wonderfully well-pitched game by Sandy Koufax, a boy I'm certain will go on to pitch many more like it and probably some even better. This boy has what it takes to become one of baseball's truly great pitchers.

"Our Reds amount to one of the best hitting clubs in the National League, but they could do nothing against the sort of stuff Koufax was throwing up there today. His fast ball was amazing, so was his curve, and he used them like a pitcher who had been around for years. I repeat, you'll see this youngster do some remarkable pitching in the years to come."

It was agreed that Hoyt should know what he was talking about. Born in Brooklyn himself, Waite, known as "Schoolboy," had pitched major league ball for twenty years. For twelve years, he was one of the stars of the New York Yankees' staff. He completed his long career pitching for his hometown Brooklyn Dodgers in 1938.

Koufax struck out fourteen men that day, the

largest total attained by any National League pitcher up to that point of the season. It bested the previous mark of twelve registered by Sad Sam Jones of the Chicago Cubs and Bob Buhl of the Milwaukee Braves.

Alston gave evidence of confidence in the youngster in this game. It wasn't until the sixth inning that the manager went out to the mound to talk to him. It happened after Sandy, with one out, had given up bases on balls to Johnny Temple and Smokey Burgess.

"I wasn't even thinking of taking him out of the box," says Alston. "I just thought that he might be trying to aim the ball and I wanted to tell him to just keep pitching as he had. I also wanted to get him to slow down a little, to take more time between pitches."

"He was great, great," remembers Campanella, his catcher. "Sandy's fastball was taking off so that the batters were hitting under it when they were hitting it at all, and his curve was great, too. And the kid wasn't a bit nervous out there. Deadly serious but not a bit nervous. He's going to be some pitcher, believe me."

Best of all, perhaps, he got a World Series share the first time out because the Dodgers won the National League pennant by thirteen-and-one-half games, then went on to take the World Series from the New York Yankees in four straight games. His share as a member of the winning set was $9,768.21. However, he didn't get into the Series as a player but he did have the best seat in the house—the Brooklyn dugout.

Sandy entered Columbia for further studies in architecture that October, turning down the suggestion that he play some winter ball in Puerto Rico, Cuba or Carribean countries with other young players.

"I plan to take one semester of work at Columbia every winter," he said. "It'll take me about four years to get my degree that way. By that time I should know whether I can make it in the major leagues."

CHAPTER THREE

KOUFAX WAS STILL a bonus baby when he reported to the Vero Beach compound the following March, but things seemed a lot different. The season before the Dodgers were pleased with him in an indulgent sort of way. Now, though he was still one of the low men on the totem pole, at least he had the feeling that he belonged. Not that his execution had changed much; he pitched a ball and it often went over the catcher's head instead of across the plate. He did it again, and again, and again.

It was another story, when Koufax made his next start. This time the opposition caught up with him in a hurry. The Milwaukee Braves knocked him out of the box in the first inning. He started again against the Pittsburgh Pirates and showed skeptics that his stylish shutout of the Cincinnati Reds wasn't a flash in the pan by whitewashing them 5-0. He permitted just five hits and fanned six.

Koufax, used in only twelve of the club's 154 games, pitched a total of forty-two innings that first season. Most of his pitching was done in batting practice or, occasionally, in the bullpen.

The Brooklyn batters were sometimes in the habit of griping when the big kid worked batting practice. They couldn't be loose at the plate, or dig in for those big practice swings with him pitching, because they never could be sure the pitch wouldn't be right at them. They were in favor of batting practice pitchers with control.

Sandy was started in five games, finished two of them and owned a 2-2 record at the season's end. That wasn't anything startling. But the youngster traveled in big league style, ate his share of king-sized ball player steaks, got to know his way around the National League, saw more movies than ever before, and made friends in the club.

This time, though, there came encouragement from coaches and players. "Come on, Sandy," they'd yell, "You can do it. Come on, Sandy boy." He grinned and tried again.

He got a lot of kidding because of his wildness, but now there was an undertone of respect, too, for they had seen how he could fire the ball. They remembered his shutouts against Cincinnati and Pittsburgh.

"Last spring I was scared and anxious," he said. "This time I'm just anxious.

"I guess the biggest difference now is that I have a feeling that maybe I belong. I've more confidence. I'm one of the players and they all know me."

He still looked like a green pitcher, still had difficulty making the fielding plays properly. When, in the drills on fundamentals, he covered first base then wheeled as though to throw home, Alston would yell: "If you don't cut away from that bag right

Sandy, the runner will knock you out of the play. Cut away."

The Dodger faculty talked about the youngster much more now than during the first spring when, if you asked a question about Koufax you had the feeling that the person being asked would say, "Who?"

"I never saw a pitcher like him, a pitcher as wild as him in spring training," said Alston. "That's the way Sandy was last spring, too. He still has trouble throwing easy.

"He has a peculiar delivery. He throws directly over his head, like a pitcher throwing a screwball. You wouldn't think a guy throwing like that would get velocity. But he can really fire that ball."

Becker, the patient pitching coach, watched him carefully and, when the fans touring the Dodger base collected around the main diamond, shunted the youngster to an out-of-sight spot behind the barracks.

"You get enough people saying, 'Wow, is he a wild one!' and you might ruin a kid," said the coach. "And we sure don't want to take a chance on ruining a kid with that kind of an arm."

"Apparently the young man is a pitching natural with built-in techniques that other pitchers acquire only through long practice and much coaching," wrote the veteran Tommy Holmes of the New York *Herald-Tribune* that second spring at Vero Beach. "That's what it must be because, including the twelve games in which he appeared as a Dodger last year, he hasn't pitched enough to have been taught much.

"Take the matter of hiding his delivery, a trick which wheels the ball halfway to the plate before either Al Campanis or rookie catcher Herb Olson could get a good look at it. All pitchers seek to acquire that extra quality known as deception and even some good ones never succeed."

All pitchers, except perhaps the outstanding pea-shooters, constantly try to improve their fastball. They experiment with overhand, three-quarter and other methods of delivery and with different grips. Koufax, however, by just doing what came naturally, made his fastball "move around" the plate. One pitch would hop, another sink, a third sail. The fastball was his best pitch but his curveball, too, was strictly major league.

In his first season Sandy didn't get a piece of a game until the Dodgers played their sixty-sixth one on June 24. In 1956 he was employed much earlier as relief; his first start was in Chicago on the club's second Western trip after the Dodgers had lost three in a row to the Cubs.

He won, giving up only five hits before being relieved in the ninth inning. In his first nine games of the new season he worked twenty-seven innings, yielding a total of twenty-seven hits and eleven earned runs. In that stretch he walked eleven men and struck out the same number.

Still, Sandy hadn't contributed much to the Dodgers' second pennant in succession. He was employed in sixteen games, just four more than in 1955. He pitched a total of fifty-nine innings. He made ten starts, twice as many as in his maiden season, but finished none of them. He had completed two the year before. He wound up the season with a 2-4 won and lost log, and his final earned run average was a lack-lustre 4.88.

No one doubted that he fired the ball fast enough to amount to a valuable pitcher some day. The question was when. "He has more than mere velocity," observed Alston one day when reporters were comparing Koufax to Van Lingle Mungo, a former Brooklyn fireballer. "Sandy's fastball seems to take off before reaching the plate. It's very hard, sometimes impossible, for a batter to follow. You have to swing a very quick bat. His ball has a fantastic rise. You sit there in the dugout and watch him and say to yourself, My, oh my, if he could only somehow learn control."

Because he had been on Brooklyn's disabled list for the first thirty days of the 1955 season, Koufax's bonus classification had been extended automatically into the first month of the 1957 season.

On May 16, Sandy ceased to be a baseball bonus child. His two years in the protection of the bonus hot-house were up. Now the Dodgers were free to ship him out for some of the experience he had missed sitting on the bench those first two seasons.

They could send him on option to a farm club in St. Paul, Montreal, Fort Worth, or Mobile. They could send him to a club in a league that rode creaky buses from town to town, sometimes, from midnight or thereabouts to dawn to make a game. They could dispatch Sandy, who had eaten as high on the hog as any major leaguer those first two seasons, to a whistle stop in Alabama where, because the price was right, the players often ate their meals in hamburger, hush-puppy and hot dog huts and on the run. And where they slept on bus seats when it wasn't in boarding-house beds.

May 16 and Alston had a surprise for Sandy. The

Dodgers were in Wrigley Field, Chicago and the manager named him the starting pitcher against the Cubs. Koufax responded with a handsome four hit 3-2 victory. He struck out thirteen men and would have made it a shutout but for two fielding errors behind him. The thirteen strikeouts gave him a total of thirty-five in his first twenty-seven innings of work in the new season.

After that, the journalists wrote, the only place Alston wanted to send Sandy was back in there to start some more games for the Dodgers. Montreal, St. Paul, Fort Worth, Mobile and Santa Barbara became just names again to the youngster, not places where he would have to work his way back.

He could unpack his bag now, Sandy thought, and not feel that he should have it ready to grab suddenly and run for the train to some farm in the sticks. He could continue to stroll into those big league hotel dining rooms, attack a king-sized steak and sign the meal check with a flourish. There was no need now to worry about the meager minor league allowance that meant hash-house food.

He could walk out to the pitcher's box at the start of a game now and feel secure because he knew there were highly-skilled infielders and outfielders backing him up, a catcher with major league credentials waiting to receive his stuff, and hitters able to produce runs for him. He wouldn't have to struggle to overcome the errors and other faults of bush league fielders, or wait in vain for his helpers to produce runs. There was even talk now of the possibility that one of the elders might move over, allowing Sandy to take his place in the regular rotation of Brooklyn's starting pitchers. Alston spoke of starting him in the next series in Cincinnati.

Things didn't, however, work out quite that way. There were some good days but a lot that turned out to be otherwise. In fact there undoubtedly were times when the high command thought it might be best after all to send Sandy down to a farm club where he could work regularly, learn his trade thoroughly, and acquire something approximating control.

His speed was blinding—yes—and he piled up 122 strikeouts in the 104 innings he pitched, but he was a thrower, not a pitcher. His wildness made it risky to put him to work as a relief pitcher when there would be men already on base when he went in.

He finished the 1957 season working in thirty-four games. The starting pitcher in thirteen of them, he was only in at the finish twice. His earned run mark was 3.89 and his won-and-lost record 5-4.

In 1958 Sandy became part of Walter O'Malley's great gold trek to California. With other Dodger pitchers he labored now in Los Angeles' huge Coliseum instead of the blue confines of Ebbets Field. No longer were they greeted like loved ones or bums—depending on their place in the standing of the clubs—by the leather-lunged Brooklyn fans.

No more would they hear the big cowbell, swung loyally throughout every home game, by Hilda Chester, Queen of the Bleachers. Or chuckle in anticipation when the manager read a note Hilda dropped to the centerfielder, "Hurry up and put in a relief pitcher."

The tumult coming from Section Seventeen behind the Dodger Dugout, where the outlandish garbed members of what broadcaster Red Barber called the Dodger Sym-phoney, would be gone. And the musicians, taking a cue from an umpire's decision against the Dodgers, would no longer play "Three Blind Mice." No more would their birthdays be greetetd happily by Gladys Goodding, the organist Larry MacPhail introduced to Ebbets Field in 1941.

They had new fans now. Fans who deserted the city, the suburbs, the beaches and the barbecue pits in great numbers to travel the freeways to see them play.

The Dodgers did beautifully at the box-office but not on the playing field. A third place team in 1957, they finished a sad seventh. Nevertheless, they could do no wrong that first season as far as the customers were concerned. There was little booing no matter how bad their performance and every Dodger feat was greeted joyously.

"It's a little fantastic," says Koufax. "The people here yell for us whether the score is 10-0 against us or 10-0 in our favor."

Sandy hit the backstop with seventeen wild pitches, just four shy of the modern record shared by Walter Johnson of the Washington Senators and Earl Wilson of the Boston Red Sox. Still he had his most productive season since the Dodgers paid his bonus. He won eleven games and lost the same number. He boosted his season strikeout total by nine to 131. He also more than doubled his previous base on balls high, walking 105.

He continued to be more sensational than successful in 1959. He blew hot and cold, inspiring predictions of sure stardom with a handsome pitching performance in one game and suspicions that he would never amount to much with a horrendous showing in the next.

In June the twenty-three-year-old Sandy struck out sixteen batters in a game in Philadelphia. He did it in the first eight innings. He needed one more to tie Dizzy Dean's National League record of seventeen and two to equal the American League record of eighteen held by Bob Feller. He couldn't, however, get any more in the ninth.

He remembered that game because he had a visitor in the middle of it.

Sandy was concentrating on a Philadelphia batter when a fan raced onto the field.

"What do you want?" said the startled pitcher.

"I bet a guy a couple of hundred bucks that I could stop the ball game."

"You stopped it all right," said Sandy. "Now how about scramming so I can get on with my work."

The exhibitionist took a whistle out of his pocket and blew it as if it was the signal to resume play. Then he departed for the detention pen under the stands with the assistance of the house cops.

"He's got a fastball you just can't see most of the time," commented Gene Mauch, the manager of the Phillies, afterwards. "He's the only pitcher around who can throw that fastball high and dare you to even foul it. Other pitchers making the same pitch would be murdered."

On August 31 Koufax finally vaulted over Dean and tied Feller when he whistled his fast one past the flailing bats of the San Francisco Giants for eighteen strikeouts during the course of an important 5-2 Dodger decision at Los Angeles.

It was a winning clutch assignment from his manager with a flourish because Sandy not only handcuffed the considerable power of the San Francisco batters with those eighteen strikeouts but also helped his club get within a game of the league-leading Giants in the National League race.

No one in the vast audience would have expected so spectacular a production after watching him work the first three innings. He struck out two in the first, only one in the second, and none at all in the third. Then starting with one away in the fourth, Sandy began to mow them down in earnest, getting fifteen of his last seventeen men by strikeouts.

At one stretch that had the fans howling at every pitch—from the fourth inning through the sixth—the youngster struck out eight straight batters before his teammates or outfielders had a fielding chance; a home run by Willie McCovey in the fifth was sandwiched among the strikeouts. Sandy wound it all up with a flourish, striking out the side in the ninth with just ten pitches.

Yet, but for a missed sacrifice bunt by the Giants, Koufax wouldn't have been able to record this great performance. With the Giants ahead, 2 to 1 in the seventh, catcher John Roseboro, led off with a single. Seeking to tie it up, manager Walter Alston ordered Maury Wills, the next batter, to bunt Roseboro to second and summoned Carl Furillo to pinch-hit for Koufax. However, when Wills was unable to advance Roseboro, the manager recalled Furillo and let Sandy bat for himself.

Two-baggers by Willie Mays and Orlando Cepeda in the first inning and McCovey's fifth inning homer had staked San Francisco to its lead. The Dodgers managed to tie the score in the ninth, 2-2.

Koufax, having struck out fifteen of the last twenty men he faced, drew a standing ovation from the crowd of 82,794 when he walked toward the home dugout after rubbing out the Giants in one-two-three fashion in the visitor's half of the ninth inning. Jack Sanford, his pitching versus, disposed of Wills to start the Dodger ninth. With Koufax the next batter, the Giants' pitcher couldn't have been less worried. Of all the pitchers in the National League Sandy probably swung the most ineffective bat.

In his freshman season he went to bat twelve times. His consistency was remarkable. He struck out twelve times. It was two seasons before he hit his first fair ball. He was an even bet to fan every time he went to the plate because he fanned his bat more often than he even fouled. His lifetime batting average was .095.

But this time up Koufax fooled everybody. He batted Sanford's first pitch to left field for a solid single. Then when Junior Gilliam followed with another single, the Giants decided to change pitchers; they called Al Worthington in to replace Sanford.

"Well, it's about time," said a caustic journalist who had been following the Giants around the league. "If that Koufax can get a base-hit, it's a sure sign that your pitcher has had it."

Wally Moon, waiting to hit in the on-deck circle, was not bothered by the mounting pressure. He walked to the dugout where Norm Larker, next in the batting order, was standing on the steps.

"You just forget all about hitting any more tonight," he said. "You might as well go back and take a seat. I've got it."

Moon drove Worthington's third pitch into the left field seats and Koufax and the Dodgers had a big, big ball game.

"You're a sweetheart," Sandy yelled to the outfielder in the clubhouse afterwards.

"That was the most beautiful game I ever saw anyone pitch," replied Moon.

"I'm glad I set a record, of course," said Koufax, sweating like a longtime resident of a steam-room, "but I'm a lot happier that we won the ball game. We've got a great chance to win the pennant now.

"You know, I don't remember a game," he went on, "in which the batters swung at so many bad balls. I couldn't for the life of me see why the Giants were going after my pitches sometimes but, man, I was glad they did."

This was the way the San Francisco batters went down, inning by inning:

First–Brandt (swinging), McCovey (swinging); second–Sanford (swinging); third–none; fourth–O'Connell (called), Sanford (called); fifth–Brandt (swinging), Mays (swinging), Cepeda (swinging); sixth–Alou (swinging), Schmidt (called), Bressoud (swinging); seventh–Brandt (swinging), McCovey (swinging); eighth–Mays (called), Cepeda (swinging); ninth–Bressoud, O'Connell, and Sanford, swinging.

Since Koufax had fanned thirteen men in his other start in Philadelphia on August 24, the eighteen strikeouts against the Giants gave him thirty-one in two successive starts, breaking Feller's 1938 record. By striking out ten more in his next assignment, a ten-inning 3-0 loss to Chicago, Sandy shattered the mark of thirty-eight in three consecutive performances shared by Feller and Walter Johnson.

The Dodgers went on to score a two-game sweep over the Milwaukee Braves, the defending champions, in the National League pennant playoff, then rode on to even greater success in the World Series that followed, defeating the American League's Chicago White Sox in six games.

Koufax could only watch while his teammates did the work in the 1955 and 1956 World Series, but this time he was an established member of the club, marked for duty.

The call came early. The White Sox, taking a 2–0 lead in the first inning, jumped all over Roger Craig, the Dodgers' starting pitcher, in the third. Nellie Fox doubled, Jim Landis singled, then Ted Kluszewski homered into the right field stands to give Chicago a 5–0 lead; that was all for Craig. The White Sox didn't stop until they had seven runs.

The Los Angeles bullpen was a busy spot. Chuck Churn had been called in to relieve Craig. When Kluszewski hit his second two-run homer in the fourth, Alston called curveball specialist Clem Labine in from the bullpen. Labine got them out but when Charlie Essegian pinch-hit for him in the Los Angeles fifth, the manager had to put another reliever to work. This time it was Koufax.

Jim Rivera became Sandy's first World Series out on a fly to center. He then made Early Wynn, the Chicago pitcher, his first World Series strikeout victim. Luis Aparicio was the third out on another fly ball.

Koufax again retired the White Sox in one-two-three fashion in the sixth; Alston sent Ron Fairly up to hit for him in the seventh. He was in the Comiskey Park clubhouse, listening to the radio broadcast of the game as it ended 11–0 for the White Sox.

The youngster was in the bullpen as Johnny Podres, with relief pitcher Larry Sherry's help, won the second game, 4–3, to even the series. He was there again when Sherry went to Don Drysdale's aid in the eighth inning and the Dodgers took the third game, 3–1. And he was still there when Sherry rescued Craig in the seventh and his team won, 5–4.

It wasn't until the next afternoon that the twenty-three-year-old lefty got his first World Series starting assignment. Everyone thought Alston would most likely start Podres, his other left-hander, and the pitcher who had beaten the White Sox in the second game in Chicago, but they guessed wrong.

"I don't want to start Podres with only three days of rest," said the manager. "He has a history of arm trouble and more rest can help him. Koufax should be ready."

Alston could also have said that Sandy's fastball, difficult for a batter to pull, was better suited to the Los Angeles Coliseum than the stuff thrown by Podres, which was more effective in the larger Chicago park. If there was to be a sixth game in the Series that's where it would be played, and the experts figured Podres would start it.

The White Sox, hoping for survival, depended on twenty-six-year-old Bob Shaw of Garden City, Long Island, unknown a few months before.

Shaw was a right-hander with a confidence that bordered on stubborness. Eighteen months ago he had been on the staff of the Detroit Tigers. When the Tigers tried to ship him to one of their minor league farm clubs, he rebelled, quitting the team and going home. The Tigers promptly traded him to Chicago, where he did nothing spectacular for the rest of the season.

The next spring he was considered a relief pitcher —not one of the better ones. Given a chance, he established himself as the club's number two pitcher, second only to Early Wynn. He finished the regular season with a better earned-run average than Wynn and an 18–6 won and lost record.

The strength of this pitcher, who grew up near where Koufax had spent four years of his boyhood, lay in control rather than overpowering speed. Shaw hadn't been at his best in losing the second game of the series to Podres, in the opinion of Al Lopez, his manager, and Sherm Lollar, his catcher. Now it was up to him to keep the White Sox from being branded World Series busts. The game meant something extra to Koufax, too. He was in the Dodger doghouse after letting his team down in a vital St. Louis game the final week of the season.

Given a 3–0 lead in the first, Sandy couldn't protect it even for one inning as he ran into his worst spells of wildness, finally giving up a grand-slam home run to Hal Smith.

Three weeks before Sandy had struck out eighteen Giants in another important game, breaking Dizzy Dean's National League mark and tying Bob Feller's major league record for strikeouts in one game. The Thursday before, though, he pitched two innings after the White Sox had put the first game of the Series out of reach. He looked fast and sharp and Alston was encouraged.

Another record-busting crowd of 92,706 sat in on this one, most of the onlookers rooting for Koufax and the Dodgers to clinch the Series.

Sandy pitched stout ball but it wasn't enough, and he lost to Shaw and the White Sox, 1–0. He allowed only five hits in seven innings, gave up one base on balls and struck out six men. He was beaten on the run Chicago coaxed out of him in the fourth inning. Nellie Fox opened it with a single, took third when Jim Landis followed with another and scored as Sherm Lollar was grounding into a double-play. Stan Williams shut out the Sox after Duke Snider pinch-hit for Sandy in the seventh, but the Dodgers could get nowhere against the pitching of Billy Pierce, relieving Shaw in the eighth, or Dick Donovan, pitcher for the ninth inning.

Koufax was a lot happier the next afternoon, however, for all he had no part in the proceedings. The Dodgers won the Series by taking the sixth game at Chicago, 9–3. Podres, the winner over Wynn, was helped again by Sherry. Each Dodger received a winning World Series check for $11,231.18.

CHAPTER FOUR

UNTIL 1960, KOUFAX didn't seem to feel that spring was the time for a young man to begin pitching winning ball games. Sandy, who normally had grown wilder than crab grass by that time of year, now seemed to be approaching a point in his career where he could discover before mid-May that the strike zone wasn't high and outside.

On April 22, he was able to win a game in the first month of play for the first time in six seasons. He did it with mid-season dispatch too, striking out eleven and allowing only three bases on balls as the Dodgers defeated the Cincinnati Reds, 5–3.

It was the twenty-first time the young left-hander struck out ten or more batters in a single game.

Koufax, who thought nothing of throwing 160 pitches or more early in the season, wound up with only 124—eighty of them were strikes. The Reds, among the better batting clubs, scored all their runs on a third inning homer by Frank Robinson and got only two hits after that.

"That pitch Robinson hit," Sandy said afterwards,

"I swear, was only about two inches from the spot I pitched to him in the eighth inning when he grounded into a doubleplay."

"Sandy has been getting a little better every spring," said Walter Alston. "And this year he's had a fine training camp and exhibition game record.

"Why I can remember the first spring he came down to us at Vero Beach, as green as any pea as you could find in a pod. You couldn't even play catch without him throwing half the balls over your head and that was only sixty feet away. It's been a good spring."

In 1960 Koufax lost more games than he won for the first time since his sophomore season, posting an 8–13 record against 8–6 the year before. Yet he was making progress. He was becoming, slowly but surely, a thinking pitcher instead of a rear-back-and-fog-it-in thrower. The improvement could be traced to a casual conversation with Norm Sherry, his roommate and the second-string Dodger catcher that spring.

Koufax was a different pitcher that afternoon. He pitched seven innings of no-hit and no-run ball, relieved because it was early in the spring and he wasn't ready to go the full nine. Sherry, his catcher, praised his unusual control.

He reached a new high in strikeouts that season, fanning 173. He began to recognize the strike zone. And he began to develop other pitches to go with his blur ball–among them a sharp curve and a change of pace. Still, his won and lost record, the sudden wild spells and other things bothered him.

Here he was in his sixth season with the club and he still wasn't the regular starter and winner he had hoped to be. Other pitchers about his own age had long since arrived.

One was Don Drysdale, the big right-hander who had been a fellow rookie that first spring at Vero Beach. In 1957 Drysdale won seventeen games and lost only nine for the Dodgers, tying for second place with 2.66 among the National League pitchers in earned runs allowed. It was a remarkable season for so young a pitcher, particularly since the club played far below the form expected of it and finished third.

Only three pitchers in the league had won more games that Drysdale that season and two of them, Spahn (twenty-one) and Bob Buhl (eighteen) were with the championship Milwaukee Braves. The other was the Phillie's Jack Sanford (nineteen), pitching since 1948.

Drysdale had been signed by the Dodgers for a modest bonus in the neighborhood of $500 when he was a schoolboy in Van Nuys, California. Like Koufax he had been an infielder, but the Dodgers decided that a shortstop who threw sidearm wouldn't do and turned him into a pitcher.

Unlike Koufax, who received a much bigger bonus, Drysdale could be farmed out. When they met in the spring of 1955, Drysdale already had a season of minor league experience at Bakersfield in the California State League. Then he picked up more knowhow with Montreal of the International League in 1955.

Koufax, bothered by his inability to level off, blamed his lack of control and other inadequacies on his infrequent starting assignments. "I know I can pitch up," he told general manager Buzzy Bavasi one day. "And I want to pitch, but I'm not getting the chance to start regularly."

"Pitch regularly?" said Bavasi. "How can you start regularly when you can't get the side out?"

"Show me a way to get the side out when you're sitting in the dugout," answered Koufax.

Suddenly, in 1961, Sandy found home plate; it no longer seemed to move on him. After seven long, disappointing years he began to enjoy the sweet smell of success.

He won eighteen games while losing thirteen, finishing seventh behind the leader, veteran Warren Spahn (21–13) of Milwaukee in the league's won-and-lost percentage.

Only Spahn (21), Joey Jay (21) and Jim O'Toole (19) of the pennant-winning Cincinnati Reds, won more games. Sandy's earned-run average per nine inning game (3.52) was better than that logged by such established pitchers as teammates Don Drysdale and Johnny Podres, St. Louis' Larry Jackson, Cincinnati's Bob Purkey, Philadelphia's Art Mahaffey, and Pittsburgh's Bob Friend.

He set a new National League mark of 269 strikeouts, while cutting his base on balls charity to ninety-six.

By June 10, he was the Dodgers' and the National League's leading pitcher with eight victories against only two losses. In beating Pittsburgh on June 10, he worked his fifth consecutive complete game victory.

The St. Louis Cardinals, a heavy-hitting lot of batters, felt like taking up croquet when Sandy beat them twice within the span of four days, allowing only three hits each time. The first was a 1–0 shutout. The second wound up 2–1, the Cardinals scoring because Koufax, reverting to old habits, balked a runner home. He struck out thirteen men, continuing his pace of almost one man an inning.

"I think I can throw the ball where I want to now," he said happily. "I'm working with a lot less effort and a lot more concentration."

His patient pitching coach, Joe Becker, also had an explanation.

"Sandy was willing to take advice and work," he said. "Toward the end of last season, he started getting his breaking stuff over the plate while keeping the ball low. We got him to shorten his stride. This year he's throwing curveballs when he's behind in the ball-and-strike count. Before this it was always the fastball. He's surprising a lot of hitters."

Among his performances were two two-hit games, both against the Chicago Cubs. He won the first 3–0 on June 20, with Ernie Banks getting a single for the first hit in the seventh and Don Zimmer getting another single in the ninth. In the second, a 2–1 job on August 29, Dick Bertell singled for the first hit in the seventh and Ron Santo got the only other hit, also a single in the ninth. Sandy was getting closer to a no-hit game.

Jim Hearn, the old Giant pitcher now a sales executive and good will ambassador for the Phillips Van Heusen corporation, had the good luck to catch Koufax's better games that season. "It's too bad the Dodgers didn't stay in Brooklyn," he says, "Then Sandy would have been a hero in his own home town.

"Not many players reach stardom where they grow up; Whitey Ford's unusual that way.

"Maybe it's just as well, though, that the club moved to Los Angeles. Otherwise, there would be an awful lot of wise guys in the stands at Ebbets Field saying they remembered when they were better pitchers than Koufax."

Hearn believes Koufax owns the strongest arm in baseball. He points out that Sandy's raw gifts are made doubly effective by his ability to pitch down to the batters from an exaggerated, directly overhand delivery.

"That's really the secret of his strikeout success, I think," Hearn adds. "There is that sharp angle from the point of release of the ball and the point of contact. You consider that angle with Koufax's jumping fastball and a curveball that seems to drop off a table.

"Then you can understand why even the best hitters in the league have so much trouble with him. You know no matter what they say about the knuckleball, the screwball, the slider and other off pitches, there is just no substitute for a good fastball thrown overhand.

"I can remember talking with some friends on the Dodgers when he first broke in. They used to tell me that he had just too many muscles, that he was the kind of pitcher who would always get strained and pulled muscles.

"They said he was Hal Schumacher's type. When Hal pitched for the Giants he used to almost vibrate himself to pieces throwing that sinker. But I don't think this will happen to Sandy. He handles himself too well."

Manager Walter Alston was naturally delighted with Koufax's arrival as a sure-enough pitcher on a regular starting rotation.

"Sandy had the ability," he says. "He just needed experience. But we always had so many pitchers that it took him six years to get the work he might have had in three or four."

"Like I said, he listens well," says Joe Becker again. "Look, when a pitcher is five runs ahead or five behind, he may get a good hitter out on something less than his best pitch. He'll think to himself, well, I've got his number now. Then the next time he's in a tight spot with the same hitter, he'll try the same pitch and get belted.

"You try to explain to pitchers how important it is to make the good hitters go for their best pitch, their 'out' pitch.

"The good ones listen and learn something. The others seem to have a hole in the head that starts in one ear and goes out the other."

Koufax, the eighteen-game winner, discussed the wasted years. "I missed that training, that experience a young pitcher needs," he told Murray Robinson of the New York *Journal-American.* "A couple of seasons in the minor leagues would probably have solved my control problem, and I might have been ready to win in the National League three or four years before I finally found myself."

The 1962 season should have been a continuation of Sandy's sudden success story, for he got off to another promising start. In a game played early in the season against the Cubs in Chicago, he equaled his strikeout record of eighteen men, first achieved in 1959, in one contest.

This jewel came on April 22 at sunbathed Wrigley Field, silencing critics who suggested that the poor lighting in the Los Angeles Coliseum was largely responsible for the strikeouts of eighteen San Francisco Giants on the night of August 31, 1959.

The Cubs went down, inning by inning like this: Elder White, 3; Lou Brock, 2; Ken Hubbs, 2; Bob Will, 2; Moe Thacker, 2; Ron Santo, Ernie Banks, Billy Williams, Don Cardwell, André Rogers, Jim McKnight and Merdith Morhardt.

A quirk of fate helped Koufax do all this. After Billy Williams hit a homer to open the ninth inning, Sandy struck out the next pair. Moe Thacker then lifted a fly to the infield. Between gusty winds and a mixed up call for the ball, Banks failed to catch it and it went for a hit. With this reprieve Koufax was able to get pinch-hitter Merdith Morhardt on a called strike for his eighteenth of the game.

By the middle of the season, it looked like another big year. He not only posted the eighteen strikeout job against the Cubs but also owned a 10–4 record, close to 200 strikeouts, an earned run average around the 2.00 mark, and a no-hit, no-run game.

This baseball bingo bit he achieved against the New York Mets (which some charged was doing it the easy way) on the night of June 30 in Los Angeles.

The score was 5 to 0, and he struck out thirteen of the league's basement boarders while walking five. The game, televised back to New York, would ordinarily have attracted about as many viewers as the weather report, but when word of what was happening spread through the bars, grills and homes of the New York area, it got a bigger audience than the late, late show.

Koufax, in his early years with the Dodgers, might have had some wild dreams about pitching a no-hitter some day. But for more than six years it seemed as though he couldn't possibly dream as wildly as he pitched.

Perhaps because he knew he had a no-hitter in the making, Koufax was a little wilder than usual. Three of the five men he walked went to first base in the last three innings, when the pressure rose.

His teammates gave him a 4–0 lead in the first inning after he had struck out the first three Mets on nine pitches, par for the course. Later, with such a prize in prospect, Sandy hesitated to take chances and became excessively cautious. They might be the Mets but he remembered staggering to a 13–4 win over them in the Polo Grounds on Memorial Day. He came close to losing a no-hitter three times.

In the second inning Frank Thomas hit a sharp grounder that looked as though it might see its way through the left side of the infield. But the shortstop, Maury Wills, dashed to his right, made an extraordinary backhand stop and just managed to throw out the slow-footed Thomas. In the sixth inning, Richie Ashburn sliced a line drive to left field and Tommy Davis lost the ball momentarily in the glare of the lights. Davis recovered in time, however, and made a fine running catch. In the ninth, Ashburn drove another to left. Davis obviously had no chance to get it and the crowd of 32,769 moaned aloud. At the last moment, however, the ball curved foul.

Koufax became the tenth Dodger to pitch a no-hitter and the first left-hander since Nap Rucker, Casey Stengel's old buddy back when they were the Brooklyn Superbas of 1908. The last Dodger no-hitter was fashioned by Sal Maglie against the Phillies at Ebbets Field in 1956. Sandy saw that one as a Brooklyn bullpen spectator.

There is something electric in any no-hitter in the making. The players sense it, the umpires and official scorers go on a nervous alert, and the groundskeepers, raking the diamond in the middle innings, pay attention to the smallest pebble.

By the seventh inning at Los Angeles, the tension was high and the customers were booing ball calls and cheering strikes indicated by Umpire Steiner when Koufax pitched. Sandy had hung up his thirteen strikeouts in the first eight innings. In the ninth he walked pinch-hitter Gene Woodling and the next three outs came on infield force-outs. He struck out everyone in the Met batting order at least once, except Thomas.

Afterwards there was the usual post-mortem in the clubhouse. And such questions as: "Was this your biggest thrill?"

"Well, I'd say it has to rank with a couple of others," Sandy answered. "Nothing will ever be a bigger thrill for me than winning my first game. I was only nineteen years old then. It was a two-hitter against Cincinnati and I think the score was 7–0.

"Then there was that eighteen strikeout game against the Giants three years ago. That was something special. I'd say those three rank about even."

Gil Hodges, Met first baseman, hit a homer against the roof in that Polo Grounds game he had just about weathered on Memorial Day. The long-ball hitting Hodges was on the bench with a damaged foot. Still, as the ninth inning neared with the New York pitcher sure to bat, Koufax was certain that Hodges would be sent up to pinch-hit by Casey Stengel.

"I sat in the dugout while we batted in the eighth," Sandy said, "and tried to figure on how I would pitch to Hodges in the ninth. I sure was surprised when Woodling came up instead. I had to start thinking all over again and I didn't have much to go on." (Wooding had done his hitting in American League.)

Woodling, a left-handed hitter rarely used against a left-handed pitcher, was also surprised when Casey sent him up to lead off the ninth.

"Grab a bat," Stengel told him. "Hittin' against this guy will be a new experience for you."

Woodling walked. It was the fifth base on balls given up by Koufax, who by now had grown extra careful.

Ashburn came next. After hitting that long one which just curved foul down the left field line, he hit into a force-play.

"Why didn't I try to bunt?" said Richie in reply to a question. "Listen, a guy with such overpowering stuff as Koufax is too tough to bunt. Your best bet is to swing away and just hope."

Koufax was now only two outs away from the jackpot. Rod Kanehl, the third baseman and fast, was the batter. He, too, banged into a force-out at second base.

Felix Mantilla, a power hitter, was next with one out. He drove one of those unpredictable high hoppers toward shortstop.

Maury Wills, anticipating the big second bounce, backed up a step. The ball went higher than he expected but the shortstop quickly shot his glove high, made the grab and threw the ball to Larry Burright at second base with deliberation, just forcing the speeding Kanehl in time. That was it.

Koufax's spectacular was witnessed by a Saturday

night crowd of 29,797. The customers made Dodger Stadium sound like a huge outdoor rock and roll arena as they thundered their applause.

"Mark that turnstile count of 29,797 well," observed Frank Finch, of the Los Angeles *Times*. "Ten years from now there will be 300,000 people who'll swear they were there. Never fails."

The month before Bo Belinsky, the rookie left-hander of the Los Angeles Angels, had pitched a 2–0 no-hitter against the Baltimore Orioles in a Saturday night game before 15,886 in the same park. When Koufax also turned the trick, it meant that Walter O'Malley's gaudy new Chavez Ravine showplace was the scene of two pitching perfectos before it was three months old.

The Dodger dressing room was a funhouse afterwards. Players laughed and joked and played baseball's ageless post-big game gags. They congratulated Sandy one by one.

Signs greeted him. One read:

June 30, 1962
Sandy Koufax's
Perfect Game.
0 for 4.
Some No-hitter!

This rib was directed, of course, at his well-known weak bat.

Another said:

Hollywood, Here
I Come.
Remember the Curfew is 5 a.m.

The second was in reference to Belinsky's after hour antics following his no-hitter.

Koufax modestly admitted that luck played its part in his achievement.

"You have to be lucky to keep twenty-seven batters from dunking one between the fielders or hitting one on the nose," he said, "and luck stayed with me.

"It was a lot tougher tying Feller's strikeout record. If you remember the first time I did it against the Giants in '59 I got into a mess of trouble right off the bat when Mays and Cepeda both doubled in the first inning."

The pitcher said he had lost control of his curveball in the middle innings but luckily managed to regain command of it in time.

The only change he made in his pitching pattern during the game was to stop throwing change-ups after the fifth inning. From that point on, he said, he had relied strictly on his fastball and curve.

"The change-up is meant to set up the batter for your other pitches rather than to get him out," he said. "I knew, of course, that I had a great chance for a no-hitter by then. So I decided that if anybody was going to spoil it they'd be hitting my best pitch doing it."

After the last New York out of the game, the Stadium scoreboard had flashed a message to Sandy and, of course, the fans.

It said that O'Malley had torn up Koufax's contract and would he please drop by the office Monday morning to pick up a better one.

"Nobody said anything to me about a new contract," said Sandy with a grin. "But I think I'll be available Monday morning."

There were other benefits besides a hike in pay, Koufax soon discovered. He was quickly offered $1,000 to appear at a testimonial dinner, and firms selling everything from shirts to hamburgers wanted to fatten his wallet for endorsing their products.

The Mets were dazzled by the young man's brilliance.

"He really opened my eyes," said Gene Woodling. "Nobody in all the years I've been playing ball ever threw one as hard as that first strike he fired at me."

"I felt he was going to pitch a no-hitter in the fourth inning," said Solly Hemus, the Mets' third base coach. "I kept needling him. 'Don't tell me it's that easy!' I'd yell. He didn't pay me the least bit of attention. Just went about his business, and, boy, business was good!"

"I knew he had his control all right," said Casey Stengel, "when he struck out my first three men on nine pitches."

It had to be Casey who made the best crack of the night. He generally held court after every game for the sports writers attached to both clubs. This time he looked around and only two writers were there.

"What happened?" he said. "Where's all them reporters tonight? Something must be going on."

The victory was the eleventh against four defeats for the pitcher. The runless game also gave him a record of having yielded just three earned runs in his last five starts for a handsome 0.63 earned run pace. He was getting harder to score against than football and Fordham's fabled Seven Blocks of Granite.

By striking out thirteen Mets the rangy southpaw made it eight times he fanned ten or more batsmen

The official box-score of Koufax's first no-hit, no-run game. Against the New York Mets at Los Angeles the night of June 30, 1962.

New York	AB.	R.	H.	TB.	PO.	A.	E.
Ashburn, lf	3	0	0	0	3	0	0
Kanehl, 3b	4	0	0	0	0	0	0
Mantilla, 2b	3	0	0	0	4	1	0
Thomas, 1b	2	0	0	0	5	1	0
Cook, rf	3	0	0	0	1	0	0
Hickman, cf	3	0	0	0	3	0	0
Chacon, ss	2	0	0	0	1	1	0
Cannizzaro, c	3	0	0	0	7	1	0
R. L. Miller, p	0	0	0	0	0	0	0
Daviault, p	2	0	0	0	0	0	0
aWoodling	0	0	0	0	0	0	0
bChristopher	0	0	0	0	0	0	0
Totals	25	0	0	0	24	4	0

Los Angeles	AB.	R.	H.	TB.	PO.	A.	E.
Wills, ss	5	0	1	1	0	4	0
Gilliam, 3b	3	0	1	1	0	3	0
W. Davis, cf	4	1	2	4	3	0	0
T. Davis, lf	4	1	2	2	2	0	0
Fairly, 1b-rf	3	1	0	0	4	0	0
Howard, rf	3	2	2	5	0	0	0
Harkness, 1b	0	0	0	0	0	0	0
Roseboro, c	3	0	1	2	13	0	0
Burright, 2b	4	0	2	2	5	2	0
KOUFAX, p	4	0	0	0	0	0	0
Totals	33	5	11	17	27	9	0

New York	0	0	0	0	0	0	0	0	0—0
Los Angeles	4	0	0	0	0	0	1	0	x—5

aWalked for Daviault in ninth. bRan for Woodling in ninth. Runs batted in—T. Davis, Howard 2, Roseboro 2. Two-base hit—Roseboro. Three-base hit—W. Davis. Home run—Howard. Stolen bases—T. Davis, W. Davis, Wills. Double plays—Gilliam, Burright and Fairly 2; Thomas and Chacon. Left on bases—New York 3, Los Angeles 10. Bases on balls—Off Miller 1 (Fairly), off Daviault 5 (Gilliam 2, W. Davis, Howard, Roseboro), off KOUFAX 5 (Ashburn, Mantilla, Thomas, Chacon, Woodling). Strikeouts—By Daviault 7 (KOUFAX 3, T. Davis, Fairly, Roseboro, Burright) by KOUFAX 13 (Kanehl 2, Cook 2, Chacon 2, Cannizzaro 2, Daviault 2, Hickman, Ashburn, Mantilla). Runs and earned runs—Miller 4–4, Daviault 1–1. Hits—Off Miller 5 in 2/3 inning, off Daviault 6 in 7 1/3 innings. Wild pitch—Daviault. Winning pitcher—KOUFAX (11–4). Losing pitcher—Miller (0–6). Umpires—Steiner, Boggess, Landes and Smith. Time—2:46. Attendance—29,797.

in a game in 1962 and thirty-nine times in his career. The thirteen strikeouts also hiked his season total to 183 in 150 innings.

Not only did Sandy seem sure to bust the National League strikeout record of 261 he set in 1961, but also the major league mark of 348 established by Feller in 1946.

CHAPTER FIVE

No ONE KNEW it but all this while Koufax was pitching under difficulties and sometimes in pain.

Early in July he found he had trouble gripping the ball when he wanted to throw a curve. He was pushing and straining, using an unnatural motion and losing his normal rhythm.

It began in a game against the San Francisco Giants just before the All Star game.

"I found that middle finger growing so numb I just couldn't spin a curveball off my fingertips," he said. "I could throw my fastball all right, so I got by throwing just fast ones and an occasional change of pace."

There was more trouble in his next start against the Mets in New York. He stiffled them for seven innings but had to quit with the Dodgers leading, 3–0. A blister had developed on the bothersome finger.

"See this swelling and discoloration on this side of the finger?" he said, showing his hand to sympathizers in the Dodger clubhouse later. "That's where it's numb. Then the pain spreads to the palm and thumb.

"It's got me stumped. I don't know how it could have started. I might have bruised it in some way, I don't know. I don't remember hurting it. I wasn't hit there by any batted ball that I remember.

"The blister? I think the blister just happened because I was holding the ball differently without realizing it.

"They tell me that it has something to do with blood circulation. They say the one thing that can help it is rest and I certainly can't do any resting now. We need all the pitching we can get."

Heat seemed to help a little. Wayne Anderson, the Dodger trainer, began applying an electric hot pad to Sandy's hand between innings.

"We hope it's nothing serious," said Anderson. "But every once in a while a certain pitch will send a twitch up his arm and that don't sound good. He complained of one tonight."

He made one more start on that trip, against the Reds in Cincinnati five days later. He had to quit after the first inning. The finger was blue, swollen and throbbing with pain which spread up his forearm.

Koufax was sent home to Los Angeles. There, after a lengthy examination by the Dodgers' Dr. Robert Woods and Dr. Robert Kerlan, his condition was described as Reynaud's Phenomenon, a circulatory affliction resulting from a blood clot in the palm. The flow of blood to the finger becomes greatly reduced. It is sensitive at first, then numb.

Dodger fans suddenly had to go shopping for medical dictionaries. Bulletins containing terms they had never met in Dodger box-scores or stories of their games, began to pop in the papers.

Reynaud's Phenomenon wasn't a spectacular young prospect discovered by a Los Angeles scout named Raymond, they learned. Reynaud's Phenomenon was a circulatory problem rare in young male adults such as the twenty-seven-year-old Koufax.

The symptoms are sometimes found in the palms of pneumatic-drill operators, they learned. The constant pounding can cause clots and loss of circulation in a localized area.

They heard the theory advanced that the extremely hard grip on the ball that Koufax used and the frequency with which he pitched caused the circulatory disorder.

The doctors disclosed the names of the four drugs they used to get his finger well again: Coumadin, Fibrinolysin, Ilidar and Priscoline. The customers at Dodger Stadium bandied the names around as though they knew them as well as any name on the club roster.

"The only time I was scared," said Koufax, "was when it was all over, the finger completely healed and the doctors told me that it might easily have gotten serious enough to be amputated if I didn't have it treated.

"I was afraid of getting a heart attack when I heard that.

"I just don't know about the future," he went on. "They say the finger will be normal again but I can't help but be a little worried about it.

"Will it come back on me, the way sore arms often do? Will it happen to me again when I pitch, this year or next or some time after that?

"So I won't think about this season, or what's left of it. What can I do about it anyway? It's gone as far as I'm concerned. I mean things like breaking the strikeout record and winning a lot of games like I did last season."

He said the Dodgers' continued success made it easier to take.

"I'm not going to second guess myself for not having the finger looked at by doctors sooner," he said, "for two reasons.

"First, it was no time to do anything that would take me out of a regular pitching turn. Drysdale and I were the only pitchers on the club winning regularly. Johnny Podres was going bad.

"I was really needed all the time, and I was getting by all right. Who knows, if I'd been out things might not have gone so well during that stretch.

"Believe me, I felt great when Podres started to do well again just when I had to stop, and the club didn't lose any games, really, with me out of the regular pitching rotation.

"The second reason is more personal. If I'd quit when I first felt that something was definitely wrong, I wouldn't have pitched that no-hitter against the Mets.

"I wouldn't have been able to help us get the lead in the race, either. And I'd be sitting out the rest of the season with a 7–2 record or something like that, and probably be no better off physically."

In the middle of the finger furor, when Walter O'Malley and other Dodger officials were getting all sorts of free advice, Jim Murray, of the Los Angeles *Times*, thought he too would try to be helpful.

"I've been wanting to speak to you about Koufax, Walt," he began.

"I know that finger of his has you worried, Walt. Well, it's on his left hand, isn't it?

"Have you ever thought of letting him pitch with his *right hand*, Walt?

"Shucks, the fingers of his right hand are okay. Right, Walt? Well then, isn't it silly to borrow trouble?"

For a long while, the Dodgers didn't let Koufax pitch for batting practice. His activities were confined to running in the outfield. He tried to take part in the sideline fun ball players call pepper games (one player bunts to four or five men standing six feet or so in front of him). He had to wear a protective bandage around a rubber sheath on the finger, however, and found he couldn't grasp the ball at all.

"I doubt if he'll be able to pitch again this season," said Buzzy Bavasi, the worried vice president of the club. "We just haven't said anything about it because we didn't want the other players thinking they'd have to do it all without him."

Walter Alston was just as glum.

"The way he's looked," said the manager, "I'd settle right now for being sure he could pitch for us next season."

The second week in September Sandy thought the finger so improved that he begged Joe Becker, the coach, for a try at pitching batting practice. He worked for almost ten minutes, throwing fastballs and breaking off curves, afraid that every pitch would have to be the last.

When it was over he walked into the clubhouse, grinning. Anderson, the trainer, came over to examine the finger.

"It looks like hell," said Sandy. "But it's all right. Honest, it doesn't hurt at all."

Koufax tried, when more batting practice trials

convinced Becker and Alston that it would be safe to use him in games, but he wasn't the same pitcher. The nine long weeks of inaction hurt.

About this time the Dodgers' pitching situation wasn't good. Larry Sherry was out of order with an injured ankle. Ed Roebuck was drydocked with a case of flu. A youngster, Phil Ortega, was too inexperienced to be risked in key spots.

They called up Jack Smith, a relief pitcher with a winning record, from Omaha. In another move that indicated desperation, Drysdale was assigned to the bullpen for possible duty as a reliever on days he wasn't being used as the starting pitcher.

They couldn't win the big ones they almost always did when Koufax was ready and able. Drysdale, though he won twenty-five games, couldn't do it alone.

They muffed a big chance on September 27. The pursuing San Francisco club lost to the Cardinals that afternoon, 7–2. Alston gave the starting assignment to Koufax that evening. But the pitcher who had been such a strong competitor months before ran out of gas. Ron Perranoski, his reliever, bowed, 8–2.

The Giants finally caught them at the wire on September 30, forcing a play-off for the National League title. A few weeks before the Giants had been virtually out of the race.

Now they went on to take the play-off and the championship—two games to one. The Dodgers were winning the third and deciding game, 4–2, going into the ninth, only to let San Francisco rally for four runs and a 6–4 decision.

Koufax couldn't help in the play-off either. Alston

started him in the first game, but Sandy quickly showed that he wasn't equal to the task.

He got the first two Giants out, then Felipe Alou doubled and Willie Mays homered. Jim Davenport led off the next inning with another homer. When Ed Bailey, the next batter, singled, Alston replaced Sandy. The Dodgers went on to lose, 8–0.

The final collapse plunged Los Angeles fans into a smog of despair. Quite naturally, most of them blamed it all on the disaster area in Sandy's left fist.

All that winter the world's most famous finger got more news space than an elephant on a tear. It had become even better known than the finger with which Ted Williams indicated his distain for Boston critics.

People kept asking: "Sandy boy, how is it?" "Howzit?" "Howzit comin' along?" on the street, in elevators, in airplanes, on golf courses, in radio and television interviews, and by medically-minded journalists in Miami hotel lobbies.

It was even asked on the stage. It became part of the act when he appeared with teammates Maury Wills, Don Drysdale, Frank Howard, Willie Davis and Duke Snider—all of them in white ties, black tails, toppers, fancy pumps and silver-topped canes—in their song and dance act at the Hotel Fontainebleau in the middle of February.

Milton Berle, heading the lavish show, would introduce them, then ask Sandy:

"By the way, how's the finger coming along?" This came up at every show.

Koufax would hold up his left hand as though inspecting it for the first time and flex the finger.

"Fine, just fine, thanks. The doctors say it shouldn't bother me at all."

The well-tanned vacationers would applaud as if for a Miami weather bureau's excited announcement that forty inches of snow had fallen in the north. So would his teammates and Berle. That bit over, the show would go on. It was schmaltz but they loved it.

The Dodgers opened their spring training at the Vero Beach compound the day after their night club act closed. It was good timing. It got them there under the wire.

Before spring rehearsals ended and the 1963 race opened, the inexperts agreed that as Koufax fared so would the Dodgers. They wrote that, barring a recurrence of his finger failure, there would be no lumps in Dodger throats come September.

As things turned out, that was about the size of it. The Dodgers started living down their sins by mid-May and moved to the front in June. They drooped a bit, then reformed to play championship ball.

By the early weeks of July, Koufax had won fourteen games, including a resplendent no-hitter against the heavy-hitting Giants, and had lost only three. With eight shutouts halfway through the season at the All-Star game break, he owned an extraordinary 1.73 earned run average per nine inning game and led the league in strikeouts with 150.

Baseball people talked about him more than ever and with increasing respect.

"I've never seen Koufax with less stuff than he had against us the other day," said Freddie Hutchinson, the manager of the Cincinnati Reds.

"He had almost nothing out there, but all we could

get was one legitimate hit and two bloopers and were shutout, 3–0."

"I know just what you mean," said Philadelphia manager Gene Mauch. "He's gotten so that he can win with ease even when he hasn't got his best stuff. That's the mark of a really great pitcher."

Koufax threw only ninety-nine pitches in his shutout of the Reds—the first time in his career he had required fewer than 100 pitches. In his no-hitter against San Francisco, for example, he threw 112.

The young left-hander, who had twice struck out eighteen men in a game, fanned only four Reds.

"Nowadays," said Sandy, "I'd rather the batter swung on my first pitch and went out. I hope to make him bite at it. The last thing on my mind most of the time is to strike out the batter."

It was about this time that the story of how a several seasons back observation made by Al Dark, the San Francisco manager, had helped Koufax become a quality pitcher. Dark, one of the thinking man's ball players, was shortstop for the St. Louis Cardinals at the time. A teammate and close friend was Wally Moon, the outfielder.

After a game in which Koufax, then a Dodger youngster of unfulfilled promise, had pitched against them, Dark noticed Sandy would bring his hands to a certain point when throwing a curveball, to another point when pitching a fastball. Dark read pitchers the way other people read books. He mentioned Koufax's giveaway to Moon.

The next year Moon was traded to the Dodgers. He told Koufax what Dark had observed.

At first Sandy refused to believe it. Other people had sometimes said that he must be tipping off his pitches but he couldn't believe that he was revealing so much so regularly.

One day in spring training at St. Petersburg, Moon arranged an experiment at a practice game in an effort to convince the young pitcher. Koufax threw ninety-six pitches while he was out there. Moon called ninety-three of them correctly. Sandy was convinced.

"Best of all," said Moon. "He did something about it. He didn't let it slip in one ear and out the other.

"That first season I played with Sandy he was just a thrower," continued Wally. "An awfully fast boy, but a thrower, and for a while it looked like he'd stay a thrower.

"Then he arrived almost overnight as far as control was concerned. He got so he could not only get his stuff over the plate but was able to spot his pitches over any part of the plate. He could get by with his fastball or stick with his curve. When he has both, the other fellows might as well shut up shop."

When the Dodgers reached the time out period for the 1963 All-Star extravaganza, it was almost the same story. Sandy Koufax was the leading pitcher in the game with a 14–3 record, and he had again thrown a no-hitter, this time against the San Francisco Giants.

Some, in fact, said that he was even better for eight of his fourteen victories had been shutouts. This gave him a fighting chance to match the major league record of sixteen set by Grover Cleveland Alexander in 1916.

He felt in grade-A condition, no longer bothered by thoughts that the costly finger ailment would flare up again.

"It took time," he said, "but my finger is absolutely normal again. The doctors tell me I have nothing to worry about at all as far as that's concerned.

"You see the trouble wasn't a circulatory disease as they thought, at all. It was due to an injury that isn't likely to happen again.

"The only trouble I've had this season was back in April when my shoulder stiffened up for a couple of days. But it came around all right."

After Koufax threw his first no-hitter against the New York Mets in 1962, some critics suggested that the feat was nothing to brag about and maybe shouldn't even be allowed to grace the record books of the game.

The Mets were such a seedy set, they said, that a no-hitter against them wasn't an accomplishment at all. Some suggested that Koufax throw the no-hitter back in, like a fisherman who has reeled in a catch under the limit.

They couldn't say that about the perfecto he pitched against the Giants on May 11 for the Giants amounted to the hardest-hitting club in the National League.

The score was 8–0; Juan Marichal was his pitching opponent, and the achievement gave him the distinction of being the second active major leaguer with two no-hitters to his credit. The other was Warren Spahn.

Like his no-hitter against the New York Mets the year before, this one was in Dodger Stadium on a Saturday night. A Saturday night game with Sandy Koufax pitching had become almost a sure sell-out —a must.

It was a Hollywood opening, an Academy Award

affair. The first ten rows always looked like the invitations had been channeled through Hedda Hopper. There would be a Doris Day here, a Killer Gray there, a Georgie Raft yonder, a Dino Martin abaft the Dodger dugout and more of the same.

There were 49,807 paid present in O'Malley's version of Grauman's Chinese Theatre that evening. More than 5,000 others got in on passes or on half-price Ladies Night tickets. The ropes were up in the Stadium's swanky eating and drinking parlors.

In his first no-hitter the previous June, Koufax walked five men. This time he allowed only two bases on balls. Perhaps the oddest feature of Sandy's sparkler was his puny total of five strikeouts, unusual because of his career average of better than one an inning.

With one out in the eighth inning, he walked Ed Bailey on a 3-and-1 pitch. Pinch-hitter Willie McCovey, who walked with one out in the ninth, was the only other San Francisco base-runner. Sandy himself attended to the final out, retiring Harvey Kuenn on a bouncer to the pitcher's box.

He made only 112 pitches to the twenty-eight men he faced. He said afterwards that he relied more on curves than his blazing fastball. He paid tribute to his companions for the support they gave him and to his catcher, John Roseboro, for doing a great job of calling the proper pitches.

The Dodgers did all the scoring he needed when Wally Moon hit a lead-off homer off Marichal in the second inning. But they belted Marichal out of the box anyway in the sixth, and added four more off reliever John Pregenzer in the eighth.

Felipe Alou gave the crowd a shock in the seventh

inning when he drove a pitch to deep left field. Tommy Davis backed up against the box-seat railing at the 360 foot mark to make the catch. Shortstop Dick Tracewski made a barehanded capture of a slow grounder by Orlando Cepeda to retire that Giant in the fifth. In the eighth Cepeda led off with a hard drive to the mount which Sandy's stab deflected to second baseman Nate Oliver, who nailed Cepeda at first by a step. Those were the only difficult chances.

As the game wore on and a no-hitter seemed very possible, the Dodgers went dumb on the bench between innings. In the seventh and eighth innings Sandy sat alone, a towel about his neck and his features grim, with no Dodger in the dugout within twenty feet of him.

"The fellows on the bench didn't want to say a thing about my possible no-hitter," he said afterwards, "but I knew it all the time. Matter of fact, I shook Roseboro off once, saying, 'Let's go with the same pitch and get this no-hit thing over with.'

"I also knew I was close to pitching a perfect game until I lost Bailey in the eighth. That must be the ultimate thing for a pitcher—a perfect game."

Koufax said he spent nearly two hours afterwards receiving congratulations. Then he went to the small FM radio station in the upper San Fernando Valley in which he owns an interest.

He had promised to appear on a fund-raising program for a recreation program for youngsters sponsored by some civic groups.

"I didn't get home until two o'clock in the morning," he said. "You'd think I'd have been bushed by then, but it was a long, long time before I finally got to sleep. After all it was quite a night."

The law doesn't say you mustn't mention the fact that a no-hit, no-run ball game is apparently in the making on the field. But there is never a whisper to that affect by the pitcher's teammates or, for that matter, the sportswriters and radio and television commentators, while the man is working in that direction.

Should someone in the press coop suddenly notice the total absence of base-hits by one team, and start to say something to that affect, he is immediately silenced.

"Waddaya' want to do, jinx the guy?" someone will say.

"Shhhhhhhhh!" others will warn, throwing their dirtiest looks at the culprit.

Usually, though, the broadcasters attached to the club being victimized by the pitcher, make no bones about the fact that the fellow is no-hitting their heroes. After all, they're not rooting against their own side. If mentioning the fact that a no-hit game is going on will jinx the other pitcher, well, good and hurray for our side.

Russ Hodges, however, is a kindly man who believes in the old traditions of the game. A broadcaster attached to the Giants since they inhabitated the Polo Grounds in New York, he was in the visitors' booth describing the game below as it was followed by the television cameras that evening in Dodger Stadium.

There was a ball game taking place, but that's about all Russ would admit out loud. Not a peep about the fact that Koufax was mowing down the Giants in hitless fashion.

Hodges devised all sorts of ways to give the play-

The official box-score of Koufax's second no-hit, no-run game. Against the San Francisco Giants at Los Angeles, the night of May 11, 1963.

San Francisco	AB.	R.	H.	TB.	PO.	A.	E.
Kuenn, lf	4	0	0	0	0	0	0
F. Alou, rf	3	0	0	0	0	0	0
Mays, cf	3	0	0	0	1	0	0
Cepeda, 1b	3	0	0	0	11	0	0
Bailey, c	2	0	0	0	9	0	0
Davenport, 3b	3	0	0	0	0	2	0
Amalfitano, 2b	3	0	0	0	0	1	0
Pagan, ss	3	0	0	0	2	5	0
Marichal, p	2	0	0	0	1	2	0
Pregenzer, p	0	0	0	0	0	1	0
aMcCovey	0	0	0	0	0	0	0
Totals	26	0	0	0	24	11	0

Los Angeles	AB.	R.	H.	TB.	PO.	A.	E.
W. Davis, cf	5	1	0	0	4	0	0
Gilliam, 2b-3b	3	2	2	2	2	0	0
Fairly, 1b	5	0	3	4	10	0	0
T. Davis, 3b-lf	4	1	1	1	1	1	0
Moon, lf	3	2	2	5	0	0	0
Oliver, 2b	1	0	0	0	1	2	0
Howard, rf	3	0	0	0	3	0	0
Roseboro, c	4	0	2	2	5	0	0
Tracewski, ss	4	1	2	2	1	4	0
KOUFAX, p	3	1	0	0	0	2	0
Totals	35	8	12	16	27	9	0

San Francisco	0	0	0	0	0	0	0	0	0–0
Los Angeles	0	1	0	0	0	3	0	4	x–8

aWalked for Pregenzer in ninth. Runs batted in—Fairly 3, Moon 2, Roseboro 2. Two-base hit—Fairly. Home run—Moon. Stolen base—Gilliam. Double plays—Pregenzer, Pagan and Cepeda; Tracewski, Oliver and Fairly. Left on bases—San Francisco 1, Los Angeles 8. Bases on balls—Off Marichal 1 (Howard), off Pregenzer 4 (Gilliam 2, T. Davis, KOUFAX), off KOUFAX 2 (Bailey, McCovey). Strikeouts—By Marichal 5 (W. Davis 2, KOUFAX 2, Howard), by Pregenzer 1 (KOUFAX), by KOUFAX 4 (Pagan 2, F. Alou, Marichal). Runs and earned runs—Marichal 4-4, Pregenzer 4-4. Hits—Off Marichal 9 in 5-1/3 innings; off Pregenzer 3 in 2-2/3 innings. Balk—Pregenzer. Winning pitcher—KOUFAX. Losing pitcher—Miller. Umpires—Steiner, Boggess, Landes and Smith. Time—2:46. Attendance—29,797.

by-play and other information between razor blade and other commercials without saying those awful two words—*no-hitter*.

"The Dodgers have four runs and nine hits," he told the folks listening back in San Francisco. "All the hits there are in the game."

Later he circled beautifully in a verbal end-around play with: "The tension is terrific here in Dodger Stadium, believe me, as everyone in the park realizes what Sandy is trying to do.

"There you see the scoreboard," said Russ as the television camera focused on the figures 0-0 in the runs-and-hits section. "It tells you a big, big story, doesn't it?"

And then: "Koufax has pitched to twenty-one San Francisco batters now and has erased all of them with the greatest of ease."

He threw out another hint. "The umpires in a game like this have a tremendous responsibility. They must be absolutely impartial.

"Ladies and gentlemen, hold everything," he said excitedly later. "Hold everything and listen to the big ovation that Sandy Koufax gets when he comes to bat. A standing ovation, folks. An ovation, I might say, that his tremendous performance here tonight against the Giants certainly merits."

The San Francsco half of the ninth inning and: "Sandy is just three outs, folks, from the record books. Just three big outs and his name will be recorded with distinction in the Little Red Book of Major League Baseball . . . Just three outs . . ."

Then: "He's done it! A no-hit, no-run game for Sandy Koufax!"

Don Drysdale said Sandy's latest no-hitter came as no surprise to him.

"I wouldn't be surprised if he pitched a no-hit, no-run game every time he goes out there," said the big right-hander. "It's only when somebody hits a ball safe off him that I'm really surprised. When Sandy's right and has his pin-point control, the other team is just over-matched."

After the game someone mentioned the fact that he had struck out only five men, an unusual low for him.

"It's not that I don't like to get all of those strikeouts," he said with a smile. "But I don't have to get them. You know that dawned on me a few years ago when I could throw just as hard as I do today, but could never be sure where the ball was going to end up.

"Joe Becker and later Norm Sherry kept pounding into me that I don't have to throw so hard all the time and the message finally got through.

"It took a long time because recognizing a fault and correcting it are two different things. I can't tell you how many hours of throwing to Becker and Sherry on the sidelines it took me to develop the proper rhythm and a really groove delivery. I'm grateful to both of them for their advise and patience."

CHAPTER SIX

WITH KOUFAX SHOWING the way, the Dodgers threatened to turn the 1962 race into a runaway. Then the Cardinals suddenly came to life and staged one of the most sensational stretch runs in baseball history.

The Cards won nineteen games out of twenty, the surge lifting them to within a one game reach of the Dodgers as the two clubs opened a series in St. Louis on September 16.

Confronted with this challenge, however, the Dodgers proved their class. They won all three games and went on to take the pennant by six lengths.

As it had during the season, the Dodger pitching proved the difference. Three left-handers—Johnny Podres, Ron Perranoski and Koufax—did the job.

Podres, who finished the season with fourteen wins against twelve defeats, won the first game, a three-hitter, 3-1. Koufax then whitewashed the Cards on four hits to win 4-0. Perranowski, the able relief jobber who wound up the year with sixteen victories and only three losses, shut the Red Birds out with three hits over six innings as the Dodgers won the third engagement in the thirteenth (6-5) to complete the sweep.

His big win in this head-on clash was Koufax's twenty-fourth of the season. It was also his eleventh shutout, a major league record for a left-handed pitcher—the most by any pitcher since Grover Cleveland Alexander, the redoubtable right-hander, fashioned sixteen with the Phillies in 1916.

His job on the Cardinals was also remarkable in that he made only eighty-seven pitches in the game. It was the first time he had thrown under 100.

Allan Roth is a sharp-eyed sleuth whose job it was to follow every pitch thrown by and at the Dodgers in every game and record them for the management's reference. He reported that Koufax had thrown a total of fifty-seven fastballs of which forty-seven were strikes and thirty curveballs for twenty strikes.

Sandy had a no-hit, no-run game in the works for six innings.

At the season's end Koufax had, besides his twenty-five victories against only five defeats, eleven shutouts, a record breaking total of 306 strikeouts in 311 innings and a league-leading 1.88 earned run average. It was the second season in a row that he led the National League pitchers in that important department.

By clinching their first pennant in four years, the Dodgers all but obliterated the memory of their humiliating collapse in 1962. The situation seemed to call for a little disorderly conduct—a clubhouse celebration awash with champagne.

But one of the most gratifying victory celebrations in the history of the club turned out to be one of the most restrained.

Perhaps the trouble was that the boys waited too long to hold their wing-ding. They actually won the pennant the week before in St. Louis when they swept the three game series with the Cardinals.

As things turned out, they clinched the pennant on September twenty-fourth before they even got to Dodger Stadium. The Cards were eliminated when they lost an afternoon game to the Cubs in Chicago.

Inning-by-inning accounts of the Chicago game were broadcast by a Los Angeles radio station. In the ninth inning the station picked up a play-by-play account direct from Wrigley Field.

This so excited John Roseboro, the Dodger catcher, that he slept right through it. Manager Walter Alston went to his dentist and was having a tooth filled when the Cubs scored the winning runs in the eighth inning.

The wildest celebration may have been the one held in outfielder Wally Moon's house.

"I was outside when my wife picked up that ninth-inning broadcast," he said. "After they gave the score, she drove to school, got kids and brought them home. We had a nice little family party to celebrate. Cokes and cookies."

Moon drove in the winning run when the Dodgers took a meaningless game from the New York Mets that night (4-1). Drysdale pitched seven innings, alowing only four hits and picking up his nineteenth victory.

"They can't say we backed into the pennant," said Alston afterwards.

"We played pretty good ball when the Giants were right on our tail and when we just had to win in that series in St. Louis.

"We might have gotten a bigger kick out of it, if we had won it right here ourselves, beating the Mets."

Casey Stengel went to the Dodger clubhouse to congratulate Alston.

"Walked over here to say congratulations so I could save the price of a telegram," said Casey.

Their pitching, spearheaded by Koufax, was the best thing the Dodgers had going for them in the World Series against the Yankees that followed.

Walter Alston's staffers led the National League with a 2.85 ERA, the first pitching group since the 1945 Cubs to be under 3.00. The Dodger pitchers authored a total of twenty-four shutouts–a club record–during the season. In ninety-nine games, they held the opposition to three runs or less.

The Big Four–left-handers Koufax and Podres, right-hander Drysdale and relief ace Perranowski–accounted for seventy-four of their ninety-nine victories.

They did not threaten the Yankees with big bats. They had gone through the season scheming and conniving, winning the pennant by speed and stealth.

They were only fourth in the National League in hitting at the end of the season, behind the St. Louis Cardinals, San Francisco Giants and Philadelphia Phillies. They were a sad sixth in fielding, ranking lower than the Milwaukee Braves, Cincinnati Reds and Phillies. Only in speed did they show the way offensively, leading the league with 124 stolen bases.

The Yankees entered the World Series as odds-on

favorites. Walter Alston surprised nobody when he announced that Koufax would start the first game for him.

The inexperts agreed that if Sandy could beat Whitey Ford, the Yankees' best pitcher, in the first game at Yankee Stadium, the Dodgers would have a good chance of winning the Series. If he failed, they said, the ogres of the American League would go on to wrap it up in their usual fashion—maybe in four straight games.

Koufax didn't fail them. He beat Ford and the Yankees 5 to 2, striking out fifteen of them along the way, a World Series record.

Off to such a resounding start, the Dodgers didn't stop. They went on to achieve what many regarded as the impossible, sweeping the Series in four straight games, with Koufax coming back four days later to beat Ford again (2-1) in the final game.

The spectacular sweep did much to make up for the past humiliations suffered by the Dodgers and the rest of the National League at the hands of the Yankees.

Pitching before a crowd of 69,000 bug-eyed spectators, Sandy let the lords of the American League know what was coming by striking out the first five men to face him. Before the afternoon was over he had fanned fifteen, more strikeouts than any other World Series pitcher before him.

Working briskly, without a full windup, he struck out Tony Kubek, Bobby Richardson and Tom Tresh in the first inning. He fanned Mickey Mantle and Roger Maris in the second before Elston Howard fouled to the catcher for the third out.

Back in the 1929 Series, Howard Ehmke—a surprise starter for Connie Mack's Philadelphia Athletics—won more or less deathless renown by fanning thirteen Chicago Cubs.

Koufax equaled Ehmke's pile when he struck out Elston Howard in the seventh and passed it when he fanned Phil Linz, a pinch hitter, in the eighth.

Twenty years after Ehmke's feat, another Dodger pitcher, Carl Erskine, pitching against another Yankee team, struck out fourteen to pass the Philadelphian's mark.

Now, ten years to the day after Erskine's game, Koufax made it fifteen. He made Harry Bright, a pinch-hitter, his fifteenth victim for the final out of the game.

Among the eight Yankee regulars, only Clete Boyer managed to get a piece of the ball every time up.

Richardson, who had always been a hot hitter in World Series competition, struck out three times; Kubek, Tresh and Mantle twice each, and all three of Ralph Houk's pinch-hitters—Linz, Hector Lopez and Bright—went down swinging.

Ford matched Koufax in the first inning, retiring the side in order and fanning Maury Wills and Willie Davis. He also took care of the ever-dangerous Tommy Davis, first Dodger up in the second. Then came trouble.

In his only other World Series start, against the Chicago White Sox in 1959, Koufax had lost (1-0). This time his teammates got some runs for him.

After Davis had struck out, Frank Howard, the huge outfielder, hit one of the longest doubles ever seen at Yankee Stadium. The ball sailed over Mantle's head, banging against a screen in front of the public address system some 460 feet from home plate.

Mantle chased the ball at top speed but had no chance to catch it. Mickey did, however, manage to retrieve it and get it back to the infield in time to hold the lumbering, six-foot, seven-inch Howard to a double.

Scarcely had the Yankees recovered from this jolt than Bill (Moose) Skowron singled through the box, scoring Howard. The Moose probably would have had to dig deep in his memory to recall a more satisfying hit—the Yankees had traded him away to the Dodgers only ten months before.

Dick Tracewski, a light-hitting utility infielder playing second base because Ken McMullen, the regular man on the job, was injured, hit another single through the box and over second base.

Then came John Roseboro, Sandy's catcher, with an unexpected shot.

Left-handed Ford threw a strike to left-handed Roseboro, whose nine home runs during the regular season were made against right-handers exclusively. Whitey threw another one and it dropped among the customers in the lower right field stands, just inside the foul pole.

Ford, the Yankee pitching bellwether for ten years and winner of ten World Series games, a record, now found himself four runs in the hole.

In the third inning he went five down. Junior Jim Gilliam opened the inning with a single and was forced by Willie Davis. When Tommy Davis singled to right field, he raced to third. Then it was up to Skowron again. This time the Moose singled to center and Willie Davis scored. The Dodgers had five runs and the Yankees none. A press-box occupant from California was appalled.

"Koufax never had a 5-0 lead," he said, "not even against the Mets. He won't know what to do with it."

From then on Koufax dominated the scene, but it wasn't all smooth sailing.

He had two out in the fifth and hadn't allowed a man to reach base when suddenly three Yankees—Elston Howard, Joe Pepitone and Clete Boyer—got singles that filled the bases. That brought up Lopez, batting for Ford. He went down swinging, Sandy's eleventh strikeout victim, to end the inning.

In the sixth, with one out, the pitcher seemed to lose some of his sharp control. He walked Richardson on a three-and-two count. The call on the fourth ball seemed to upset him and he also walked Tresh.

Here was the grand opportunity for the Yankees—the next two batters were Mantle and Maris. But Sandy got Mantle on a pop to Tracewski and Maris on a pop to Wills and pop went the threat.

That seemed to take all the starch out of the Yankees, though they recovered to wrench away what had promised to be a sure shutout from Koufax in the eighth.

With one away, Kubek beat out a hit to deep shortstop. Richardson struck out for the third time, but Tresh homered into the lower left field stands. Mantle then drew a base on balls but Maris couldn't get the ball out of the infield.

In the ninth, with one out, Pepitone got his second hit of the game, another single. Koufax finished strong, however, getting Boyer on a fly and Bright for his fifteenth strikeout.

"I got a little bit tired about the fifth inning," Sandy said afterwards, "but then I seemed to get my strength back. I felt strong at the end."

"His elbow started to tighten up on him a little, that's what it was," said Joe Becker, the pitching coach. "That's been happening to him on and off all season. It's nothing new or serious.

"But when it happened today, Sandy began to press out there. He tried to reach back for something extra to put on the ball. That caused him to take too big a stride and it destroyed the rhythm of his motion.

"He decided to forget about his curveball after that," continued the coach, "and stick to his fastball. That's practically all he threw, with some change-ups, for the rest of the game."

"He's had a cold and that probably had something to do with his getting tired," said Alston. "He hadn't pitched since last Wednesday when he shut out the Mets for five innings.

"Sandy always keeps himself in good shape, but with this cold he hasn't done as much running as usual. Maybe that, along with working faster than he usually does, bothered him.

"Ordinarily, he doesn't run out of gas. Many a time he's pitched stronger ball in the eighth and ninth innings than in the first and second."

Someone asked Sandy if he had thought about the World Series strikeout record.

"Not until they put out that message about fourteen strikeouts on the scoreboard in the ninth," he said. "Then I thought it sure would be nice to get another one, but the main thing was to win the game."

Just then Erskine walked into the clubhouse to congratulate his former teammate on breaking the record he had set ten years before.

"Actually I gave the record to Sandy publicly last year," said Carl, "but he got hurt and couldn't collect. So, really, he let me have one extra year on in the record book.

"I'm delighted that he's kept it in the Dodger family. I think he's the man who deserves it. He's just about the greatest strikeout pitcher of them all, isn't he? You know something? He may break it again before this series is over."

"When I got my fourteenth," said Sandy, almost apologizing to Erskine, "I thought to myself: Maybe that's enough and I ought to leave it there.' "

The Yankees, who had found out that Sandy Koufax was for real, had some nice things to say about him. In typical fashion, though, they refused to rate him in a higher category than any other pitcher in baseball.

"There are some other guys who pitch pretty well against us," said Houk, the manager. "Some days we don't get any runs."

"You don't know how fast he is from the papers," said Tresh, "but it's too soon for me to say he's the greatest around."

"Don't forget the screen in centerfield was down today," said Richardson, "and the background wasn't good for the hitters. When it's down, any fastball pitcher who throws overhand will give you a lot of trouble."

"Sure I knew I was his fifteenth strikeout," said Bright. "I saw it on the scoreboard. I didn't want to strike out, that's for sure. I wanted somehow to get on base. But I don't think anybody will remember me for what I did today.

"I wait seventeen long years to get into a World Series and I strike out," he continued. "And as if that isn't bad enough, 69,000 people were rooting against me, hoping I'd strike out."

Someone asked Pepitone, who got two hits, if he thought he'd do better against Koufax the next time.

"Yeah, yeah, yeah," said the first baseman. "He's the kind of a pitcher you see once an' get a couple of hits an' then don't want to see ever again."

Mantle struck out his first two times up, popped to the second baseman and walked. Once he threw his batting helmet to the ground in disgust.

"He let me get off the hook twice," said Mickey. "He had two strikes on me my last two times up. He might have struck me out and made it sixteen or seventeen.

"He threw me a half a dozen pitches that were right down the middle an' I felt sure I could hit them. But I kept foul tipping them off. I guess his fastball must go up."

"One good thing about it, anyway," said Howard. "He can't pitch every day."

"Everything I read or heard about him was true, all right," said Yogi Berra.

Koufax's fifteen strikeouts went this way: Richardson 3, Kubek 2, Mantle 2, Tresh 2, and then Maris, Pepitone, Lopez, Howard, Linz and Bright.

Johnny Podres, just as left-handed if not as fast, took up where Koufax had left off in the second game at the Stadium as the Dodgers won again, 4 to 1. They scored twice in the opening inning off Al Downing and that proved to be enough.

Podres held the Yankees to six hits in eight and one-third innings. They broke into the run column only in the ninth when Hector Lopez doubled and Elston Howard scored him with a single off reliever Ron Perranowski.

As Podres mowed them down, the Stadium scoreboard flashed the intelligence that the Yankees had hit a total of 152 home runs in 155 World Series games.

"Yeah, that so?," said one fan. "Where are those home run bats now?"

They were still asking the whereabouts of that famed Yankee power after the third game, for this time Don Drysdale, a right-hander, shut them out, 1-0.

A Los Angeles crowd of 55,912 exulted as Drysdale blanked out the Yankees with three hits. Two were singles by Tony Kubek. Mickey Mantle got the third when he bunted over the onrushing Gilliam's head.

Drysdale piled up nine strikeouts, getting Mantle, Elston Howard, Tom Tresh and Jim Bouton twice and Clete Boyer once.

Bouton pitched almost as well. He yielded only four singles in seven innings, but gave up five bases on balls. The first walk, to Gilliam in the opening inning, proved his undoing since it led to the lone run of the game.

The Yankee pitcher got Willie Davis out on a fly to the right fielder but he then made a wild pitch on which Gilliam reached second. When Tommy Davis slashed a hit off Richardson's leg, the ball bounded into right field and Gilliam scored.

Next afternoon they got another treatment from Koufax. Toiling and spinning through the bright autumn sunshine, the slender southpaw held them to six hits and struck out eight as he won the fourth game that meant the World's Championship for the Dodgers, 2-1.

Whitey Ford was even stingier, confining Los Angeles to two hits. If it hadn't been for Howard, in fact, Whitey would have had a no-hitter. The big outfielder singled in the second inning for the Dodgers' first hit. In the fifth he put them ahead (1-0) with a tremendous drive deep into the second tier of the left field grandstand.

Not since 1905, when every game was a shutout—three by Christy Mathewson of the New York Giants, one by Chief Albert Bender of the Philadelphia Athletics and one by Iron Man Joe McGinnity of the Giants—had the pitching lodge dominated the competition for the baseball championship the way the peggers took over the sixtieth World Series.

In many ways, the 1963 Series was a throwback to the old days. Not only did the pitchers dominate things but Alston employed only thirteen players in licking the proud New Yorkers. At the end the Yankees owned a team batting average of only .171. The Dodgers didn't knock down any records with their bats either, their mark being .214.

Up to the seventh inning of the fourth game, Mantle had been one of the Yankees' foremost flops. His only hit in the first three had been a bunt that sailed over the head of the onrushing third baseman and he had struck out four times.

"Mantle and all the others thought they were seeing and hitting the ball," Roseboro had said after Koufax's first win, "but they weren't. It would go by them. You could hear Mantle grunt, 'unngh!' as he swung and missed."

Now, though, Mickey earned his pay. He struck a long home run into the left field pavilion in the seventh inning to tie up the game (1-1). Elston Howard followed with a single, but Koufax pitched his way out of trouble.

Up to this point the Yankees, for all their ineptitude, had not made a mistake on the field. Now they made a big one and before the dust had settled, the Dodgers had the world's championship.

Jim Gilliam led off the Los Angeles half of the seventh with a high hopper to the left side of the infield. Boyer timed his leap perfectly and came down with the ball.

The third baseman took a step, then fired the ball to Joe Pepitone. The throw was on target but Joe muffed it completely. He later said he lost sight of the ball against the background of the white shirt-sleeved crowd.

By the time Pepitone had caught up with the ball, Gilliam was on third. Willie Davis, the next batter, brought him home with an entirely adequate fly to centerfield. Mantle caught the ball and made a strong and accurate throw to the plate but Gilliam raced across yards ahead of it with what proved to be the winning run.

It was the Yankees' turn to get a break in the ninth but they were unable to take advantage of it.

Bobby Richardson opened the inning with a single. The meatier part of the New York batting order now came up, but Sandy reached back for that something extra. Tresh, after faking a bunt, swung and missed. He then took two more strikes on sharp-breaking curves.

Mantle also looked at a ball which started outside,

but curved over for a third strike. Wills then made a fine stop of Howard's grounder to his left but his throw to force Richardson at second was dropped by Tracewski.

The tying run was now on second base but Koufax saw that it stayed there. He threw a high fastball to Lopez. The Yankee tried to check his swing but couldn't get his bat away in time. The result was a slow tap to shortstop. Wills raced in for it, threw to Skowron at first in plenty of time, and it was all over.

Never, in twenty-seven other autumns as the American's League's best, had the Yankees lost a four game series, and the way they managed so completely to lose this one was called beyond belief.

Their vaunted power never showed up. Between Tresh's two-run homer in the eighth inning of the first game and the one Mantle hit off Sandy in the seventh inning of the fourth, they sent ninety-four batters to the plate without one hitting the ball into the seats.

Now, they beat a hurried retreat out of Los Angeles with their heads still high and nothing but praise for Koufax—who whipped them twice—and Johnny Podres and Don Drysdale, the pitchers who stopped them in the middle games.

Alston could afford to be a gracious winner.

"We just caught the Yankees when they were in a batting slump," said the Dodger manager. "They are a great team."

"Ford was pitching such a tremendous game, I didn't think we'd get a second run off him," said Koufax. "I said to myself, 'This thing isn't going to end in nine innings.' "

He thought the home run pitch to Mantle was something of a mistake.

"It was supposed to be a fastball inside. But I didn't get it inside far enough.

"I didn't want Tresh to bunt the man to scoring position in the ninth, so I kept the ball high. He struck out on a high curveball. It wasn't a good pitch, really. I was just as glad he didn't swing at it."

"He's a great pitcher," said Mantle before leaving. "You know both his curve and his fastball start out the same way—way up here. You just have to set yourself for a fastball against him or you have no chance at all.

"Halfway to the plate, you still don't know for sure what the pitch is—fastball or curve. If it's a fastball, it looks like it's going too high, so you don't swing. But then it turns out to be a curve and it breaks down out of nowhere over the plate. By then it's too late to swing. He's just a tremendous pitcher, that's all.

"I can see why he almost always pitches a low run game. His strikeout totals must be high all the time.

"When a pitcher has you missing the ball completely so much, there's less chance of errors ruining his win. He also cuts down the chances of sacrifice flies killing him. Another thing, he seems to be at his best when there's pressure on. He always has something extra to call upon."

CHAPTER SEVEN

BEFORE GOING TO the Dodger's big victory celebration Koufax drove to the Yankees' hotel in downtown Los Angeles to visit Roger Maris, knocked out of the Series by a left arm and elbow injury when he banged into a railing trying to field a drive in the third inning of the second game.

The other Yankees had already left on their chartered flight back to New York, but Maris had gone back to his hotel before flying to his Missouri home.

The brevity of the Series did not affect the players' pool, which was limited to the first four games. The pool went over the million dollar mark for the first time—$1,107,546.43. Sandy, one of the twenty-nine on the Los Angeles club to receive a full share, got a check for $12,794.00.

There was a bronze Oldsmobile in the two-car garage attached to Koufax's Studio City home. In mid-October it was joined by a Corvette sports car, awarded to him by *Sport* magazine as the outstanding player in the 1963 Series.

Koufax was named Male Athlete of the Year in an

Associated Press poll that winter. Roger Maris, Maury Wills and heavyweight fighter Ingemar Johansson hadn't fared well after being named in previous AP polls.

Wills, named Male Athlete of 1962 after establishing a major league record by stealing 104 bases, had been held to forty in 1963.

Johansson won the award in 1959 after he knocked out Floyd Patterson to win the heavyweight championship. The following year the big Swede was flattened by Patterson.

Maris won the honor in 1961, the year he hit sixty-one homers and broke the record for a single season. In 1962 the Yankee outfielder hit thirty-three home runs.

"It doesn't worry me at all," said Sandy. "Matter of fact I haven't even thought about it."

Koufax outdistanced two of the top quarterbacks of the football season in picking up the 1963 Male Athlete of the Year award. They were Y. A. Tittle of the New York Giants and Roger Staubach of Navy. His selection capped a long list of honors received for his sensational pitching feats.

The Baseball Writers Association of America's special selection committee—two from each National League city—voted the swift throwing left-hander the National League's Most Valuable Player Award. He was also voted the major league pitchers' Cy Young Award.

The New York chapter of the Baseball Writers Association voted him the Babe Ruth award, given the outstanding player of the World Series. *Sporting News*, the baseball bible, named him Player of the Year.

There were other scrolls and trophies presented with appropriate speeches at luncheons and banquets on the rubber chicken circuit all winter. He went to Rochester, New York one night to be presented with the $10,000 Hickok Belt, awarded to the year's outstanding athlete.

It was bound to happen. In Los Angeles, Civil Service Commissioner Ike Greenberg, stood up and demanded that the city change the name of "Fairfax Avenue" to "Koufax Avenue."

Sitting on a dais at one affair after another, Koufax listened to a lot of tributes.

"There's no doubt about it," said Stan Musial, the super hitter of the St. Louis Cardinals. "This year he's the best pitcher in the game."

"We did better against him than any other club," said Bobby Bragan, the manager of the Milwaukee Braves, "because he only beat us once.

"We didn't beat him but we got him out of the ball game the other five times he started against us. We have a lot of good right-handed hitters like Mathews and Torre and Aaron and Crandall. That gave him a little trouble.

"I don't mean to say that we had his number or anything like that. When he has his stuff there's no such thing as having his number.

"He might run around next season and beat us five or six times. That's the way he is. When he's got it, that's all, brother.

"He's the reason you never saw the Dodgers in much of a losing streak. He was their stopper. He won for them every fourth day."

"Instead of a 25-5 record, he might have wound up with 35-4," said a Dodger team mate.

The man had something there. In one of his losses, 1-0 to the Cincinnati Reds, he allowed only three hits, one a bunt, and struck out ten men before going out for a pinch-hitter in the eighth inning.

He pitched exceptionally well in six other games in which he was neither winner nor loser.

He pitched a two-hitter with five strikeouts through six and two-thirds innings, a seven hitter with eight strikeouts through nine and one-third innings, a nine-hitter with ten strikeouts through twelve innings, a five-hitter with six strikeouts through eight and two-third innings, a four hitter with eight strikeouts through seven innings and an eight hitter with ten strikeouts through seven and two-thirds innings.

His shutouts solved the problem when Dodger bats sputtered, as they often did that season.

One of his record-breaking eleven was the no-hit, no-run game against the San Francisco Giants. Two of them were two hitters. Five were three hitters. Two were four hitters. In his other shutout he held Milwaukee to six hits.

As Bragan noted, when Koufax had his stuff, it was good-bye. It had been all of that to the Giants and then to the Cardinals when he blazed through the final six weeks of the race.

On August 29 he beat the Giants, 11-1. Eight days later in San Francisco, he beat them again, 5-2. And then there was that 4-0 decision over the Cardinals on September 17. His five September wins had kept the Cardinals at bay.

One night in Forbes Field, Pittsburgh, before the Dodgers went on to their big series in St. Louis, was memorable.

The scoreboard suddenly showed two runs for the

Cardinals in the first inning. Behind the Dodger dugout, a fan saw it and yelled:

"The Cardinals got two runs in the first inning with Bob Gibson pitching!"

Wally Moon heard him and poked his head out of the dugout.

"Yeah," he said, pointing to the scoreboard, "and the Dodgers got one in the first with Koufax pitching!"

Sometimes, at these baseball banquets, question and answer time followed the speechmaking.

"What about the new strike zone, it's bigger. Did it make a difference?," he was asked.

"No, no difference as far as I was concerned," answered Sandy. "You pitch to the hitter, not to the strike zone."

"What's the best pitch in your opinion, a real good fastball?," asked another.

"Yes, a good fastball," Koufax replied. "But you need breaking stuff, a curveball too, because most of the better hitters are fastball hitters. They dare you to throw it."

"Hey Sandy," one yelled. "Name us the best hitters in the National League. The ones who give you the most trouble."

"Well, Henry Aaron of Milwaukee's the best fastball hitter in the business for my money. He can murder your very best pitch any time. Then there's Willie Mays and Orlando Cepeda of the Giants and Frank Robinson of the Reds and Dick Groat of the Cardinals. And, of course, there's Tommy Davis of my own club."

The record-busting pitcher didn't think the night club work in Las Vegas and Miami and the banquet appearances he made from coast to coast and even in Canada, would lead to a letdown in 1964.

"I've been careful about my weight and my rest," he assured the Dodgers when he signed a new contract for a reported $70,000.

"I arranged the banquet appearances so that I could get a couple of days off in between each appearance. And I never stuffed myself. Sometimes I'd just nibble at the appetizer at those big dinners and that was all. I'd have my regular meal before that."

Two former Brooklyn catchers, Steve Lembo and Joe Pignatano, met Sandy again when he attended the New York Baseball Writers annual eating and oratorical contest that February.

Lembo still scouts for the Dodgers while he works as one of the Abraham and Straus department store executives in Brooklyn. Pignatano serves as a coach for the Washington Senators, managed by his old Brooklyn teammate, Gil Hodges.

"We had quite a reunion," said Lembo afterwards. "Joe roomed with Sandy one of those early seasons and they had a time remembering things.

"We both had to agree he had matured tremendously in recent years. He was in a rough spot in the beginning since he was a bonus kid and taking up a place on the roster an experienced player might have filled. And he went all those years learning how to pitch without being able to get into enough games to give him the experience he needed. He really learned how to adjust himself to conditions.

"One thing Joe pointed out is that Sandy has really mastered the new high strike zone. It must be frustrating for a batter to have Sandy get two strikes on him and then pinpoint that fastball at shoulder level.

"His fast one rises but the batter can't afford to take the pitch. When he swings, he either pops it up or strikes out."

Koufax shut out the Cardinals (4-0) in the opening game of the 1964 season, but the Dodgers lost their next seven games. Sandy again led the National League pitchers in won-and-lost percentage with nineteen wins against five defeats for a .792 mark and a 1.74 earned run average, but it wasn't enough.

The Dodgers, world's champions and four-straight conquerors of the mighty Yankees in 1963, were not only dethroned but went tumbling to a sixth-place tie with Pittsburgh.

Lack of punch, an inadequate defense and injuries all contributed to the club's shocking flop. Alston's forces never rose above seventh place until they deadlocked the Pirates on the closing day of the season.

On the club's first road swing, when the Dodgers were trying to end a long losing streak, Koufax started against the Cardinals in St. Louis and only lasted the first inning.

From the start, he didn't look at all like the twenty-five game winner of 1963, using slow stuff to get the first two batters. Then he made a third strike wild pitch past Bill White, who was able to take first base.

Ken Boyer walked on four straight pitches, a sure indication it wasn't the old Koufax, and then Charley James unloaded a three-run homer.

He managed to get the next man for the third out but failed to start the second inning.

"He was visibly hurt when he threw that wild third strike," said Dr. I. C. Middleman, the Cardinals' team physician. He described Koufax's injury as an elbow inflamation and slight muscle tear in the left forearm.

"He has some swelling on the inside of the forearm," said the physician. He doubted, though, that there was any damage to the cartilage in the elbow or calcification or bone chips.

"His injury isn't unusual for a curveball pitcher," Dr. Middleman added. "It's a tricky type of an injury and could be dangerous without proper care."

"It hurts like anything," said Koufax afterwards, disclosing for the first time that he had been troubled by the elbow for about three weeks.

"I haven't had anything on the ball in any of my starts. I was just lucky enough to get by with it, however, until tonight, when it really got me bad."

A medical case again, Sandy was flown back to Los Angeles, where he was examined by Dr. Robert Kerlan, the club's orthopedic specialist.

The doctor gave him injections in the strained area around the elbow and the upper part of the forearm, then another injection where the tendon attaches to the bone. He also began treatments with ice packs, hot whirlpool baths and ultra sound.

Koufax was on the shelf for eleven days, much to the distress of the Dodgers, who couldn't help but remember how the circulatory ailment in the index finger of his pitching hand sidelined the left-hander after fourteen victories in 1962 when the Dodgers were in first place. The Dodgers wound up losing the pennant to the San Francisco Giants in a play-off.

On May 5, Sandy made his first start since that painful April night in St. Louis. Los Angeles hopes rose again when he pitched a three-hit, thirteen strikeout, 2-1 decision over the Chicago Cubs.

He walked three Cubs and let only one get past second base. The exception was André Rogers, who tied the score with a home run in the eighth. Maury Wills won it for him with a single in the tenth inning when Dick Ellsworth walked Dick Tracewski and then hit Koufax with a pitch.

It was the fifty-second time in his career that Koufax struck out ten or more in a game. The major league record of fifty-four was held jointly by Rube Waddell and Bob Feller.

On June 4, a sports page headline in a Los Angeles paper screamed:

NOBODY'S PERFECT – SANDY WALKS ONE!

Koufax had struck again, pitching the third no-hit no-run game of his career against the Phillies in Connie Mack Stadium, Philadelphia.

The score was 3 to 0 and the big win came at an appropriate moment for the Dodgers' situation was getting serious. They had been beaten two straight games by the Phillies and another defeat would have dropped them into ninth place.

Sandy's third no-hitting nugget put him right up there in some pretty illustrious company. Only three other pitchers had been able to fashion three hitless, runless games—Larry Corcoran of the Chicago National League club in 1880, 1882 and 1884; Cy Young of the Cleveland American League club in 1897 and the Boston Red Sox in 1904 and 1908; and Bob Feller of Cleveland in 1940, 1946 and 1951.

He threw white bullets at the Phillies, striking out twelve of them. And he was the acme of efficiency, using only ninety-seven pitches. Only four balls were hit to the outfield.

By now it was a baseball saying that you could tell early on how Koufax would pitch. This night everyone knew it was going to be one of his special games by the way he set the Phils down in the early innings.

He struck out one in the second, then two in the third and went on from there. The Phillies struck out this way: Triandos, Taylor and Short twice each; Allen, Callison, Cater, Amaro, Wine and Seivers.

The lone Philadelphia base-runner was Richie Allen, who walked on a three-and-two pitch in the fourth inning. The fourth ball was a low fastball and Sandy said afterwards that there was no doubt about the call by Plate Umpire Ed Vargo. Allen was out stealing on a fine throw by catcher Doug Camilli.

Allen also made the Phillies' best bid for a hit when he hit one of those high bouncers toward third in the seventh. Jim Gilliam charged the ball and got his man at first base on a close play. Danny Cater's line drive to Wes Parker, the right fielder, in the eighth inning was Philadelphia's only well-tagged shot.

With two out in the ninth, Bobby Wine fouled a pitch into the dirt and the ball bounced up and struck Vargo in the throat.

The umpire was shaken up but took only a little time out.

"I not only wanted to finish the game," he said, "but I didn't want Koufax to cool off. He was red hot, going great at the moment."

Things hadn't been going as well for Koufax as some sideline observers liked. He had to spend a lot of time denying stories that his finger or arm was bothering him again. He had some well-pitched games and others that weren't so well done.

Before the game, he told dugout visitors he had been studying pictures a magazine had taken of his motion.

"I think I know now what I've been doing wrong," he said. "I'm stepping too far to the left with my right foot and coming across my body. I'm blocking myself out and hurting my rhythm. I've got to open up my motion more.

"This was the best one of them all," he said of his third no-hitter.

"Sure, it's always a great thrill. I used to think that striking out those eighteen men was the greatest, but it can't top pitching a no-hitter.

"It's like that fifty game hitting streak Joe DiMaggio had one season. If you miss nineteen you have to start from scratch again.

"I guess a fellow starts thinking about the possibility of a no-hitter when he's finished warming up for a game. Every time I start I think of it. I know I'm not going to pitch one every time out but you never know if that first hit will beat you—I just don't want to let them get it.

"When you're in the middle inning of a game and they've got no hits, you're bound to start feeling the pressure. You try to pitch a little harder.

"Then, there's always the crowd and the way it sounds. Here the crowd is against you, as it should be. But you know in the ninth inning, when we were leading 3–0, they wanted to see me get the no-hitter."

The crowd of 29,709 was the largest so far that season in Philadelphia. There were groans when Frank Howard hit the three-run homer that won the game in the seventh, but they changed to cheers as Sandy finished his brilliant job.

Koufax's third no-hit, no-run game against the Phillies at Philadelphia, the night of June 4, 1964.

Los Angeles	AB.	R.	H.	TB.	PO.	A.	E.
W. Davis, cf	4	0	0	0	1	0	0
Wills, ss	4	0	1	1	0	2	0
Gilliam 3b	4	1	1	1	0	3	0
T. Davis, lf	4	1	2	2	1	0	0
Howard, rf	3	1	1	4	1	0	0
Fairly, 1b	1	0	0	0	3	0	0
McMullen 1b	3	0	1	1	7	0	0
Parker, rf	1	0	1	2	1	0	0
Camilli, c	4	0	0	0	12	1	0
Tracewski, 2b	3	0	1	2	1	0	0
KOUFAX, p	3	0	1	1	0	2	0
Totals	34	3	9	14	27	8	0

Philadelphia	AB.	R.	H.	TB.	PO.	A.	E.
Rojas, cf	3	0	0	0	1	0	0
Callison, rf	3	0	0	0	2	0	0
Allen, 3b	2	0	0	0	1	0	1
Cater, lf	3	0	0	0	1	1	0
Triandos, c	3	0	0	0	6	0	0
Sievers, 1b	3	0	0	0	12	0	0
Taylor, 2b	3	0	0	0	2	2	0
Amaro, ss	3	0	0	0	2	8	0
Short, p	2	0	0	0	0	2	0
Roebuck, p	0	0	0	0	0	0	0
Culp, p	0	0	0	0	0	0	0
aWine	1	0	0	0	0	0	0
Totals	26	0	0	0	27	13	1

Los Angeles	0	0	0	0	0	0	3	0	0	–3
Philadelphia	0	0	0	0	0	0	0	0	0	–0

aStruck out for Culp in ninth. Runs batted in—Howard 3. Two-base hits—Tracewski, Parker. Home run—Howard. Double play—Taylor, Amaro and Sievers. Left on bases—Los Angeles 4, Philadelphia 0. Bases on balls—Off KOUFAX 1 (Allen). Strikeouts—By KOUFAX 12 (Callison, Allen, Cater, Triandos 2, Sievers, Taylor 2, Amaro, Short 2, Wine), by Short 4 (Howard, Camilli, Koufax, Wills), by Culp 2 (Gilliam, T. Davis). Runs and earned runs—Short 3–3. Hits—Off Short 8 in 6 2/3 innings, off Roebuck 0 in 1/3 inning, off Culp 1 in 2 innings. Winning pitcher—KOUFAX (6–4). Losing pitcher—Short (3–3). Umpires—Vargo, Forman, Jackowski and Crawford. Time—1:55. Attendance—29,709.

The baseball beat was still buzzing over the twenty-eight year-old pitcher's latest classic when the Dodgers arrived at Shea Stadium, New York, their next stop.

Koufax was honored before the game with the Mets by the members of the Tomahawks, the Bensonhurst boys' team he had once played with, the sports writers and the New York club.

Deployed around home plate, twelve of the Tomahawks—some of them with a lot less hair and a lot more weight than when the team won the championship of the Ice Cream League from the Scorpions in 1952—talked over old times.

"We'd have never won the championship if it wasn't for our star pitcher," said Stan Siegel, the second baseman. "And you know we really expected him to become a big leaguer."

"He had everything," said Lennie Gross, who should know since he was the team's catcher.

"You mean Sandy Koufax, of course," a photographer said.

"No," answered Joe Siegel, Stan's twin brother and the Tomahawks' shortstop. "We mean Mike Fields. He was the greatest pitcher the Tomahawks ever had. But he wanted to become a doctor, so he never got serious enough about baseball to be interested in any major league offers."

"Where's Mike Fields now?" someone asked.

"He got tied up at the hospital," said Hal Laufer, the centerfielder who became an insurance broker. "He had to perform an emergency operation. He's at Coney Island Hospital."

So Mike Fields, who won twelve games and lost only one in the Ice Cream League that year, missed the ceremonies honoring Sandy Koufax, the sometime first baseman who lost the only game he started for the Tomahawks.

M. Donald Grant, the Mets' Chairman of the Board, presented Sandy with a plaque on behalf of the club; Jack Lang, secretary-treasurer of the New York Chapter of the Baseball Writers of America, presented the Babe Ruth Award to the outstanding player of the 1963 World Series, and Jimmy Murphy, one of the founders of the Ice Cream League, presented the Helping Youth Award.

The award, its people said, went to Koufax because of his many personal appearances on behalf of youngsters as well as in recognition of his decorous conduct on and off the field. The Helping Youth Award turned out to be a handsome nineteen inch high affair of wood and brass. A picture of the Tomahawk team was mounted on the base with the figure of a pitcher in motion on the top.

It was the only figure of a pitcher they could find, said a member of the committee, and he hoped Sandy wouldn't mind that the figure was right-handed.

"Anyway," he said, "It looks for all the world like Mike Fields."

On June 17, when he shutout the Milwaukee Braves (5–0), Koufax's won-and-lost record stood at 9–4, which could be compared favorably to his 10–3 record of exactly a year ago, when he had gone on to bag twenty-five games and virtually every pitching honor in baseball.

It was his fifth straight victory and his third shutout in his last four starts. No enemy runner had crossed home plate on him in two weeks. He held the Braves to three hits and struck out eight to regain the National League strikeout leadership with 100.

On August 8, while beating Tony Cloninger and the Braves, 5–4 at Milwaukee, he jammed his left elbow while sliding into second base. The Dodgers, remembering the past, shuddered in their dugout. Nevertheless, Sandy went on to win a 4–1 game at Cincinnati four nights later, then blanked the Cardinals 3–0, at St. Louis, August 16. With nineteen victories, he had the most wins of any pitcher in the majors.

The pain kept coming back to his elbow after each effort, however, finally forcing him out of the regular four-day pitching rotation. One victory away from becoming a twenty game winner again, the left-hander did not pitch for more than two weeks, hoping that rest would help. He tried to warm up before a game in St. Louis on August 30 and had to stop. "It feels worse than ever," he told manager Alston.

Later general manager Buzzie Bavasi called the ailing pitcher. "There's nothing you can do to help yourself or the club there," Bavasi said. "You'll be a lot better off here in Los Angeles."

Bavasi said the probable loss of Koufax would be a big blow to any chance they had of salvaging third or fourth place.

"But we have to think about Sandy first," he said. "We can't take the chance of ruining his career."

Back in Los Angeles Koufax got the final word—no more pitching that season.

"It's something that won't respond quickly," said

Dr. Robert Kerlan, the club physician. "It's going to be a gradual thing. It won't clear up until the season is over."

Despite the two long lay-offs because of the arm and elbow trouble, Sandy's chart for the season showed 223 strikeouts in the same number of innings, and seven shutouts—more than any pitcher in the league. He had an eleven-game winning streak going before being done in by a ninth inning fielding error in a game against the San Francisco Giants, July 26. He didn't lose another game.

By leading the National League in earned run average for the third straight year, he tied Grover Cleveland Alexander's record. Alex led the league with ERAs of 1.22, 1.55 and 1.85 in 1915, 1916 and 1917. Koufax did it with 2.54 in 1962, 1.88 in 1963 and 1.74 in 1964.

Sandy showed up for contract signing ceremonies in the club offices on December 17 with Don Drysdale, Willie Davis and Tommy Davis. The highest salaries, estimated in the neighborhood of $75,000 each, went to Koufax and Drysdale. The biggest raise, an estimated $10,000 went to Willie Davis, putting his salary in the vicinity of $30,000.

Koufax said the sore elbow that sidelined him for the final six weeks of the season was sound again, but that he wouldn't test it until spring training. "If I hadn't tried to come back too soon, I probably could have pitched the last couple of weeks," he says. "But when a pitcher has nineteen wins, he's anxious to make it twenty, and I tried to pitch too soon. I just wouldn't quit until it was too late.

"Maybe if we'd had a chance, if we were in the

thick of it, I might have been able to pitch one more game down the stretch. I couldn't have pitched more than that one, though."

"I asked Dr. Kerlen if he would have given Sandy permission to pitch if we needed him," says Buzzy Bavasi, "and he told me he definitely would not have allowed it. He said Sandy could have damaged his arm so badly he might not ever be the same pitcher again."

CHAPTER EIGHT

THIS WAS THE SPRING of 1965 and for four seasons now Walter Alston, counting his assets before the Dodgers began to play for keeps, ticked off Koufax's name first. Then he said a prayer that, for the first time since Sandy had become a quality pitcher, the left-hander would not be plagued by arm trouble.

After finding himself in 1961, eighteen victories to thirteen, Koufax went on to handsomer won-and-lost charts (his record over the past four seasons was 94–38) and greater earned run averages than any other living pitcher. There wasn't another pitcher around with a higher ratio of strikeouts for innings pitched; he struck out 1,396 batters in 1,317 innings.

Historians of the game couldn't help but think of what Koufax might have done if he'd been in good shape during that stretch. He might have gotten 300 to 350 more strikeouts a season, piling up to perhaps 1,800 strikeouts.

"I've never seen a pitcher with his build," says Anderson, the Dodger trainer. "He probably has the strongest shoulder muscles of any pitcher in the business." The man who rubs down the Dodgers went on to point out that Koufax has big feet (he wears size 13 ½ shoes), big hands, and unusually strong back muscles.

"He doesn't look husky when he stands out there on the mound—just a little over six feet, and tall and lean," says Anderson. "But he fools people. He weighs 200 pounds—all muscle.

"I have to rub him with hot oil every game he starts. Those muscles can tighten up at any time. The hot oil fights off the wind and the evening chill. It's like a channel swimmer covering himself with oil before jumping into the ocean."

Anderson also rubs Sandy's arm after every game. The terrific strain of pitching changes the normal flow of blood. The strain can also tear muscles; when this happens the blood collects at the trouble spot. Rubbing the arm toward the fingers draws the blood down and away.

Early in the spring of 1965, Koufax was throwing as if the perplexing elbow trouble, which had finished him for the last month of the 1964 season, had disappeared for good. But late in the training period the pain returned. He was flown from Vero Beach to Los Angeles on April 1. An examination disclosed that he had, of all things, an arthritic condition in the elbow. Alston was told to forget his plan to start the left-hander against the Mets in the opening game at Shea Stadium on April 12.

"Sandy has a traumatic arthritic condition," said Dr. Robert Kerlan, the club physician. "It tends to flare up in the left elbow under repeated stress.

"It's too early to tell what the results of treatment here will be and too early to tell when he can pitch again. I'm not going to be overly optimistic.

"He's at the peak of his career now, but remember this—he's been throwing hard for ten years."

Asked if he knew of other pitchers able to continue pitching despite such a condition, the doctor said: "Yes, quite a few have. It depends on the degree of the ailment.

"There is no cure for arthritis, but we may be able to get him to where he can play."

Dr. Kerlan said he had treated a number of pitchers with arthritis in the major and minor leagues, though he declined to name them. The orthopedic specialist also said there had been some who were forced to quit.

Since pitchers cannot escape repeated stress, the news of the latest Koufax ailment cast a lot of gloom over the Dodgers he left behind in the Vero Beach camp—just after he remarked he had never felt better. His work in the exhibition games seemed to bear him out. In five games and thirty-eight innings he had an ERA of 3.00. In his last two starts he had gone eight innings each time with impressive effectiveness.

"I felt the best I had all spring the last day I pitched," he says. "But the next day back came the pain."

General manager Buzzy Bavasi began to look like a genius. He had been quoted as saying that he traded Frank Howard, the huge, homer-hitting outfielder to Washington for Claude Osteen, a fine left-handed pitcher, because he anticipated the possibility of Koufax breaking down. "Sandy's elbow injury last August was the compelling reason that we dealt for Osteen."

On April 6, Koufax—treated with cortisone, heat and physio-therapy until the swelling in the elbow was reduced—was given permission by Dr. Kerlan to rejoin the club. He made his first start of the season on April 18. A cold, mean wind blew across the field in Philadelphia. It wasn't the ideal day for a pitcher with a history of arm trouble, but Sandy went all the way to beat the Phillies, 6–2.

He struck out seven men and at times threw as hard as he ever did, but he tired, his control was erratic, and noticeably, he didn't sidearm left-handed hitters. "I'm cutting out the sidearming because I want to eliminate irritation as much as I can," he explained afterwards. "It may have been part of what brought on arthritis." Still he held the Phillies to five runs, their two runs on the scoreboard put there by the line drive homer Dick Stuart hit in the sixth inning.

John Roseboro, his catcher, praised Sandy's pitching. "He was a bit wild–high now and then–but he was buzzing the ball. His speed was up to par. I didn't call for one change-up all afternoon. He had a struggle, sure, but not because his elbow was giving him trouble. His control was off and he was going to three-and-two on a lot of hitters. But he was still throwing hard."

Four nights later in Los Angeles, Koufax, back in his old rotation, beat the New York Mets with a nine strikeout four-hitter. Sandy knew he'd be able to pitch soon after he woke that morning. He knew it would be all right because he was able to reach for the alarm clock without any trouble.

"I know when I've got it," he said ("it" being arthritis). "The elbow locks on me and that's it. When it's bad I know it's bad. But I never know at what time it'll happen.

"Most of the time it's happened when I was asleep

after I'd pitched a game. The pain would wake me up.

"I felt as good pitching against the Mets as I've ever felt. I wasn't too happy about my control and I wasn't crazy about my curve ball, but they'll shape up. The curve is usually the last to come."

He blamed lack of work rather than the arthritis for the slowness with which he was rounding into shape.

"This Mets game was one I had to have under my belt. It'll be a lot easier the next time because I should be able to throw the ball where I want to and not smack down the middle."

Apparently he was well again with no sign of his old ailment. In the first eight starts he did not deviate was in his old strikeout groove, too. On April 30 he was shaky, allowing the Giants five runs in seven innings and striking out only seven, but then he moved on with eight, eleven and thirteen strikeouts in his next three starts–the last a ten and one-third inning game against Houston.

It was his fifth win in seven decisions and upped his strikeout total to seventy-four, best in the majors.

"The doc can't get over it," said Sandy. "My arm is far better than he thought it could be. You know it was only a while back that they were saying, well, maybe I would be able to pitch once a week instead of every fourth day.

"I was almost willing to settle for that. After all it meant twenty-five starts."

Koufax would pitch and hope and the morning after he'd awaken expecting the elbow to be as big and round as his knee instead of its normal size.

"I often thought of staying up all night to watch it," he said. "I thought that if it did blow up, they could get it under control and I'd be all right even if I did miss a regular turn. But in the last three starts it's been better than ever."

The Dodgers were doing well at this point because Sandy was back on the beam. It was a team that had to rely on quality pitching because it had a hard time scoring runs. When they lost Tommy Davis, the outfielder and one of their legitimate hitting streaks, many thought that would be the end of them. But it wasn't.

"It's like 1959 all over again," said Koufax. "Seems that whoever is in left field gets the big hit for the big run that's just enough to win. Look at the other night. Al Ferrara comes off the bench to hit a three-run homer. It's our only hit of the game and we win, 3–1.

"Going all season without a lot of runs can be a big strain on a pitching staff. But remember that we have four pitchers who might just beat you, 1-0."

The Dodger dandy became the major league's first fifteen game winner with a 4-2 decision over the Pittsburgh Pirates on July 11. With the season thirteen weeks old he had yet to miss a turn. In twenty-one starts he had fourteen complete games. His 169 innings were the most any pitcher had worked and his 15–3 won-and-lost record and 169 strikeouts were tops in those departments.

Yet rumors that his elbow was acting up continued. He had won seventeen games by July 29, but the word spread that he was in trouble again when he lost a 4–1 game to the Cincinnati Reds that night.

Dr. Kerlan examined the elbow as he did after every game and found it somewhat swollen.

"He's had a flareup," said the doctor. "I would say

that the arthritic condition, which is chronic, is a bit worse."

Koufax pitched eight innings, struck out eight, allowed five hits and walked one.

In the early innings the stiffness appeared. Sandy took massage treatments for it on the bench and in the clubhouse between innings. He was somewhat irked over the fuss made over the flaring joint.

"I had trouble getting loose and my control was bad," he said, "but that's nothing new.

"After you go nine innings consistently your arm has a tendency to become tired. Sometimes it comes back even stronger after you've been knocked out in the fifth or sixth inning."

He had won eleven straight games before this loss to the Reds. Moreover, even in losing, he had at one stretch retired thirteen Cincinnati batters in a row so he thought the furor "utterly ridiculous."

By now Sandy had learned to live with his arthritis. He was helped by doctors, masseurs, pills, ointments and an ever-ready pail of ice. After pitching a game, he slipped his left arm into a cellophane sleeve and dipped it into the bucket of shaved ice. This was now standard treatment for the elbow which stiffened and swelled after games, reacted sharply to temperature changes, and gave off the nagging pain of arthritis.

When he beat the Milwaukee Braves 6-3, for his nineteenth win of the season on August 6, they began to say Sandy would be the first pitcher to win thirty games in one season since Dizzy Dean did it in 1934, the year before Koufax was born.

"Having nineteen wins this early in August," said Gene Oliver, the Braves' first baseman, who collected three of the seven hits the Dodger fireballer allowed, "is like hitting .450 in August. I'd say with an average like that you'd have a heck of a chance to hit .400.

"It's got to be fun for him to pitch," said the appreciative Oliver. "He's got such great stuff he can laugh the whole game.

"He'll make a mistake and you'll get a hit off him and he'll look you over and laugh because he knows you're not going to score any runs. I guess it's the relaxed feeling you get from being a winning pitcher."

Koufax, the picture of intensity as he stares at the batter, denied he was a laughing boy out there.

"It's fun," he admitted," but it's also hard work."

It was also more fun than it used to be when he had a bat in his hands.

One day in last August he sat in the Dodger dugout during the last of the ninth inning of a game with the Houston Astros. There were two out and the score was tied, 2-2.

Jim Lefebvre got a base on balls and then Jim Gilliam was walked intentionally in order to get at the next batter–Koufax.

Alston, with the top of his batting order due up in the tenth inning, decided to let Koufax hit.

"Here's where I help myself," said Sandy, and he did just that. He hit the first pitch into left field to win his own game, 3-2.

On September 10 in Los Angeles, it came time for Koufax to crank up his arm a few extra times and pitch his annual no-hit, no-run game. This time, proving that practice makes perfect, he made it a faultless job in beating the Cubs, 1-0.

He retired in order the twenty-seven batters he

faced, and struck out fourteen, the seventy-ninth time in his career he fanned ten or more in a game. The fourteen whiffs lifted his major league leading total to 332.

It was something very special, the first perfect game of his sparkling career, the eighth in modern baseball history and only the third in National League annals, following Jim Bunning's perfecto against the New York Mets in 1964.

He also eclipsed all multiple no-hit pitchers. Bob Feller who pitched no-hitters in 1940, 1946 and 1951 was the only other modern pitcher to have as many as three.

At the start the fans in Dodger Stadium could have been excused for wondering if it was going to be one of Sandy's off days.

His first pitch bounced into the dirt four feet in front of the catcher and for the first few innings he threw nothing but curve balls in an effort to loosen the muscles of his arthritic arm.

The arm soon responded and he began to use his fastball, too. The crowd of 29,139 began to buzz as the Cubs walked to the plate, took their big cuts and walked back to the dugout again.

He struck out the last six batters he faced and seven of the last nine.

In the eighth he had to meet two of the Cubs' hardest-hitting players—third baseman Ron Santo and first baseman Ernie Banks. He struck out both and completed the inning by fanning Byron Browne, rookie left fielder.

As tension mounted in the ninth, he fired a third strike past Chris Krug, the young Chicago catcher. Pinch hitter Amalfitano went down swinging;

then it was up to Harvey Kuenn, another pinch-hitter and a former American League batting champion. Kuenn also went down swinging and Koufax had his perfect game.

Bob Hendley was the losing pitcher and he threw quite a game himself. The Dodgers scratched out the only run of the game in the fifth inning on a walk, sacrifice, stolen base, and an error. But the first hit of the game didn't come until the seventh inning, when the Dodgers' Lou Johnson hit a bloop double into left field with two out. There was no other hit.

"It's a shame Hendley had to lose a game like that," said Sandy afterwards, "but I'm glad we got that run or we'd have been out there all night.

"I think the stuff I had was my best of the season. I had a real good fastball and that sort of helped my curve."

He said certainly he was aware that he had a no-hitter going.

"You always know," he said, "but you don't particularly pay any attention to it early in the game. But in the seventh inning I really started to feel that I had a shot at it."

Walter O'Malley, the Dodger owner, gave Koufax his annual $500 no-hit, no-run game bonus for the fourth straight time.

"I suppose," he said, "someone will say that Sandy deserves a million dollar contract."

They asked Dr. Kerlan if the arthritic condition in the pitcher's elbow had changed.

"No," replied the club physician, "he hasn't had a normal arm at any time this year. I'm sure he didn't have one tonight. It just proved you can pitch a perfect game with an arthritic elbow."

The Perfect Game
(Box-score)

CHICAGO (N.)

	AB	R	H	TB	PO	A	E
Young, cf	3	0	0	0	5	0	0
Beckert, 2b	3	0	0	0	1	1	0
Williams, rf	3	0	0	0	0	0	0
Santo, 3b	3	0	0	0	1	2	0
Banks, 1b	3	0	0	0	13	0	0
Browne, lf	3	0	0	0	1	0	0
Krug, c	3	0	0	0	3	0	1
Kessinger, ss	2	0	0	0	0	2	0
Amalfitano, a	1	0	0	0	0	0	0
Hendley, p	2	0	0	0	0	0	0
Kuenn, b	1	0	0	0	0	0	0
Total	27	0	0	0	24	10	1

LOS ANGELES (N.)

	AB	R	H	TB	PO	A	E
Wills, ss	3	0	0	0	0	2	0
Gilliam, 3b	3	0	0	0	0	1	0
W. Davis, cf	3	0	0	0	2	0	0
Johnson, lf	2	1	1	0	2	0	0
Fairley, rf	2	0	0	0	3	0	0
Lefebvre, 2b	3	0	0	0	1	0	0
Traceweski, 2b	0	0	0	0	0	0	0
Parker, 1b	3	0	0	0	4	0	0
Torborg, c	3	0	0	0	15	0	0
Koufax, p	2	0	0	0	0	0	0
Total	24	1	1	2	27	3	0

Chicago	0	0	0	0	0	0	0	0	0–0
Los Angeles	0	0	0	0	1	0	0	0	x–1

a) batted for Kessinger in ninth. b) batted for Hendley in ninth. Two-base hit–Johnson. Struck out–by Koufax 14, Hendley 3. Bases on balls–by Koufax 0, Hendley 1. Winning pitcher KOUFAX. Losing pitcher HENDLEY. Umpires–Vargo, Pelekoudas, Jackowski and Pryor. Time 1:43.

The History of Perfect Games

Year	*Name, Club and Date*	*Score*
1880	John Lee Richmond, Worcester vs. Cleveland, NL, June 12	1-0
	John W. Ward, Providence vs. Buffalo, NL, June 17	5-0
1904	Cy Young, Boston vs. Philadelphia, AL, May 5	3-0
1908	Addie Joss, Cleveland vs. Chicago, AL, Oct. 2	1-0
1917	Ernie Shore, Boston vs. Washington, AL, June 23	4-0
1922	C. C. Robertson, Chicago vs. Detroit, AL, April 30	2-0
1956	Don Larsen, New York, AL, vs. Brooklyn, NL, Oct. 8	2-0
1964	Jim Bunning, Phillies vs. New York, NL, June 21	6-0
1965	Sandy Koufax, Los Angeles vs. Chicago, NL, Sept. 10	1-0

The perfecto was Sandy's twenty-second win. He figured to get nine more starts before the end of the season and, by winning eight of them, could become the first National League pitcher to win thirty in thirty-one years.

He lost the next one, however, bowing to Hendley of the Cubs this time. He was in five more games before time ran out, starting and winning four of them, three in shutout style.

One was a 2-0 job on St. Louis for the Dodgers' eighth straight win; in it he recorded his 356th strikeout of the season, breaking Bob Feller's nineteen-year-old record.

The lean lefty topped Cincinnati, 5-0, on Wednesday, September 29, allowing only two hits and recording thirteen strikeouts. More important, it opened the Dodgers' first place lead over the Giants to two games with only four games left to play.

It was the Dodgers' twelfth straight win and meant that they needed only to win three out of four from Milwaukee to clinch the pennant.

Minnesota had already clinched the pennant in the American League and the World Series was scheduled to start in the Twins' Bloomington stadium the following Wednesday. Wednesday was Yom Kippur, the Jewish Day of Atonement and Koufax doesn't play baseball on Yom Kippur.

"I'm praying for it to rain Wednesday in Bloomington," Sandy said. "Then I can pitch the opening game on Thursday."

Saturday, pitching with only two days rest, Koufax fogged the ball past Milwaukee for a pennant-winning 3-1 win, his twenty-sixth of the season. He allowed but four hits and fanned thirteen, giving him a record-busting season total of 382.

The victory, the Dodgers' fourteenth in their last fifteen, climaxed a comeback that brought them from four-and-a-half games behind San Francisco to their third pennant in seven years and their seventh in the last fourteen.

They won it in typical Dodger fashion. They made only two hits, both by second baseman Lefebvre. One of their runs scored on a wild pitch, the others on bases on balls.

Speaking just a decibel above a whisper, a weary, perspiring Koufax confessed that he had about reached the end of his endurance when he retired Dennis Menke of the Braves for the last out in the ninth inning.

"I'm tired, very tired," he said. "I don't remember ever being so tired in my life. I feel like I'm 100 years old."

The count on Menke went to 2-2. Koufax, using no windup, reared back and fired a reasonable facsimile of his noted fastball. Menke raised a long fly to Lou Johnson in left field.

"I thought that ball was never going to come down," Johnson told Koufax afterwards. "But when it did—boy, did I squeeze it!"

"It goes without saying that I'm terribly happy we won the pennant," said Sandy. "But you know what I'm most thankful for?

"I'm most thankful for not having to miss one start all season long.

"I'm grateful that I was physically able to pitch. Even when I had a good arm, I was missing one or two starts every season."

CHAPTER NINE

THE DODGERS WENT into the World Series with a team batting average of only .245, lowest ever for a National League pennant winner. They had to scratch for runs all season long.

"They won it with two pitchers–Sandy Koufax and Don Drysdale–and a guy who swiped bases like crazy," said the gagsters. They parlayed speed, the bunt, and pitching to win the pennant by two games.

Walter Alston didn't mind the jokes. To him they now sounded good. And the odds-makers made his club look the same way. Despite the fact that Minnesota's musclemen led the American League in hitting, won the pennant by seven games, and were playing the first two games before a friendly crowd in a park with familiar, friendly fences, the Dodgers were a 11-10 choice to win the opener and a 7-5 favorite to win the Series.

Buzzy Bavasi, Dodger general manager, liked their chances too. He predicted his boys would sweep the Twins in four straight.

"The Dodgers are in for a surprise," Sam Mele, the

Minnesota manager, retorted. "He's got our guys a little disturbed by his comments. They're all fired up."

"What was I going to tell a guy who woke me up after I had only a few hours sleep after our victory party?" said Bavasi. "I was half asleep. I said the first thing that popped into my head. I said we'd win it four straight."

The Dodgers made a poor prophet out of Buzzy from the start. They lost the first game to the Twins, 8-2. Don Drysdale was knocked out in the third inning. Zoilo Versalles, a wiry 150-pound Cuban, stunned him with a three-run homer, drove in a fourth run with a single in the sixth, and stole second base on a pitchout.

Meanwhile Jim (Mudcat) Grant, whose 21-7 record led the American League pitchers during the regular season, pitched steady ball though afterwards he said he thought it was one of his poorer games.

"I was terrible," said Mudcat. "I didn't have a curve, a changeup or a slider. I just sort of escaped."

Angelenos, stunned by what they saw and heard of the opener on their television sets, were in for an even greater shock the next day. This time the Twins beat Koufax, 5-1. Like Drysdale in the opening game, he didn't reach the seventh inning.

Jim Kaat, only twenty-five, turned in a superb job with a seven-hitter while the Dodgers' defense collapsed with three errors. Jim Gilliam, the thirty-six-year old coach who returned to action at third base in May, opened the gates in the Twins' two-run sixth inning with a two-base error.

Koufax allowed six hits and two of the five runs. He struck out nine. Although he gave up only one

BOX SCORE OF 2nd SERIES GAME

Los Angeles (N)	AB.	R.	H.	RBI.	PO.	A.	E.
Wills, ss	4	0	1	0	1	2	0
Gilliam, 3b	4	0	0	0	0	0	2
W. Davis, cf	4	0	0	0	1	0	0
Johnson, lf	4	0	0	0	3	0	1
Fairly, rf	4	1	2	0	1	0	0
Lebebvre, 2b	4	0	2	0	2	0	0
Parker, 1b	1	0	1	0	4	1	0
Roseboro, c	4	0	1	1	11	2	0
Koufax, p	2	0	0	0	1	2	0
a-Drysdale	1	0	0	0	0	0	0
Perranoski, p	0	0	0	0	0	0	0
Miller, p	0	0	0	0	0	0	0
b-Tracewski	1	0	0	0	0	0	0
Totals	33	1	7	1	24	7	3

Minnesota (A)	AB.	R.	H.	RBI.	PO.	A.	E.
Versalles, ss	5	2	1	0	0	0	0
Nossek, cf	3	0	1	0	4	0	0
Oliva, rf	4	1	1	1	3	0	0
Killebrew, 3b	3	0	2	1	2	1	0
Battey, c	4	0	1	0	3	1	0
Allison, lf	4	1	1	0	2	0	0
Mincher, 1b	4	1	1	0	7	4	0
Quilici, 2b	2	0	0	0	1	3	0
Kaat, p	4	0	1	2	5	0	0
Totals	33	5	9	4	27	9	0

a-Struck out for Koufax in 7th.
b-Lined out for Miller in 9th.

Los Angeles (N)	0 0 0	0 0 0	1 0 0—1
Minnesota (A)	0 0 0	0 0 2	1 2 x—5

LOB—Los Angeles (N) 8, Minnesota (A) 8, 2B—Oliva, Allison. 3B—Versalles. S—Nossek, Parker.

	IP.	H.	R.	ER.
Koufax (L)	6	6	2	1
Perranoski	1-2/3	3	3	3
Miller	1/3	0	0	0
Katt (W)	9	7	1	1

BB—Koufax 1, (Quilici), Perranoski 2 (Killebrew, Quilici), Katt 1 (Parker). SO—Koufax 9 (Battey, Allison 3, Mincher, Katt 2, Versalles, Oliva), Perranoski 1 (Katt), Katt 3 (Johnson, Drysdale, Fairly). HBP—By Katt (Parker). WP—Perranoski. BALK—Perranoski. U—Venzon (N) Plate, Flaherty (A) First Base, Sudol (N), Second Base, Stewart (A) Third Base Vargo (N) Left Field, Hurley (A) Right Field. T—2:13. A—48,700.

base on balls, Sandy said his high breaking stuff was too wild.

"He's just as tough as I expected," said Harmon Killebrew afterwards. "It's definitely a big lift to beat him."

"I think the knowledge that I was pitching against Koufax relaxed me," said Kaat. "Working against a guy like that tended to take some of the pressure off me. I know nobody expected me to beat him. That helped.

"After watching him for about two innings I thought we'd never get a run off him. I know he's a great pitcher but I tried to forget about that and just concentrate on the Dodger hitters."

There were reports that the pitching mound in the Twins' Bloomington stadium was too flat and had hampered both Drysdale and Koufax. The Dodger pitchers, however, weren't talking about it.

"No excuses," said Sandy. "My control was off."

"I just couldn't get the ball where I wanted it," said Drysdale.

Gene Mauch, the manager of the Phillies and a spectator at the Series, remembered, however, that Koufax had trouble with the mound during the All Star game there in July.

"He wasn't stepping off the rubber like he usually does," said Mauch. "He walked guys."

The fans were still in a state of shock when the Series moved on to Los Angeles for the third game but an old Dodger named Casey Stengel wasn't.

The Perfessor sluffed off the fact that only three times in the history of this annual best four-out-of-seven tournament had a team rebounded from two straight defeats to win the Series.

"When I was with the Yankees, we were down the first two games and came back to win," said Casey. "They can do it too. But they'll have to shake off their shock to do it.

"I got great respect for the Twins and to judge them now they're playing the same way the Dodgers did all year, but the Dodgers are a long way from being finished.

"There's no question in my mind but that Koufax is the best pitcher in baseball even though he got licked the other day.

"He averaged over a strikeout an inning this season an' that's just plain amazin'. I don't know of anyone else who ever did it over such a stretch."

The Dodgers' Hollywood fans turned out in force on their return. The ham wasn't all confined to the concession counters or eating parlors in O'Malley's playpen.

Milton Berle and Dave Chassen shared dugout level box-seats that put them eyeball to eyeball with the players—in this case the Minnesota Twins in the adjoining dugout.

Doris Day, resplendent in a bright green outfit, sat in the next box, eating a hot dog and posing for pictures with Jim Grant, the Twins' pitcher, and others. Uncle Miltie, of course, grabbed an even bigger hot dog and elbowed his way into the background.

The Dodgers, though, play second fiddle to nobody as public personalities. The entire ball club starred in Berle's half-hour television documentary on the Dodgers over the weekend. In another show Koufax was lionized as never before. And Maury Wills, who also sings, signed for a personal appearance at Lake Tahoe after the Series.

Koufax, just warming up, drew the largest crowd on the field before the game. The interested onlookers included Elmer Valo, the former outfielder, covering the series as a special writer for the Allentown, Pennsylvania *Morning Call.* Toward the end of his career Valo played for a spell with the Philadelphia Phillies. He faced the rookie Koufax twice and walked both times. The ham coming out in him as though he had inhabited the Hollywood scene for years, Valo couldn't resist the temptation to grab a bat and square off at the plate as Koufax heated up his arm.

"That's right, grab a bat, old-folks," Sandy said amiably, "and I'll hang a curve for you."

Valo did and Koufax threw a curve that broke more than a foot across and down. Valo, appearing unimpressed, called back innocently, "What was that —your slider?"

Then Claude Osteen, the left-handed pitcher Bavasi had traded big for when he suspected Koufax's arthritis might let him out of the season, came through in the grand manner to put the Dodgers back in contention.

Some cynics had begun to think of a Minnesota sweep instead of the four straight Dodger decisions Bavasi had brashly promised.

If Drysdale (23-12), and Koufax (26-8) couldn't stop the Twin's thumpers, what chance was there for an Osteen whose season's won-and-lost was 15-15?

The buck-toothed, crew-cut pitcher changed all that, making Smogville, California, unload all the praise words in the dictionary with a five-hit, 4-0 decision over the American League larrupers who had demolished their darlings, Drysdale and Koufax.

Osteen, a left-hander from Tennessee's branch

water country (Caney Springs is the post office address) tamed the Minnesota maulers with a sinkerball pitch that seldom got higher than a batter's toes.

"Me, I just can't overpower 'em like Koufax an' Drysdale," he said, "so what I do is try an' get them to hit the ball into the ground.

"Nope, this wasn't the best game I pitched," he went on. "You may not believe this but my best game was against the New York Mets. An' you know somethin'? I got beat, 1-0."

The largest crowd (55,934) to see a game at Chavez Ravine rooted the heroes home. The Dodgers were able to play their old aggressive, racy style of play behind Osteen because they were never behind.

"We were able to run," said Alston happily. "In Minneapolis we were four or five games behind each game and just couldn't.

"I talked to the players before the game," he continued. "I reminded them about the 1955 Dodgers and how they bounced back after losing the first two to the Yankees. I told them they'd been able to win the pennant then because they weren't afraid to be daring on the base paths, and that they should go right on that way."

It's a rough assignment for a batter faced with hitting off Don Drysdale when the pitcher is what the trade calls "right." Drysdale was his old self for the fourth game–big, overpowering. He allowed only five hits and struck out eleven in reversing his first game loss to Mudcat Grant, 7-2. The big Cat couldn't last through six innings this time out. He gave up six hits and five runs, including Wes Parker's home run in the fourth.

The Dodgers were jackrabbits again as they made

six infield hits that included three bunts, stole two bases, were caught stealing twice, and harried the Minnesota infield into a pair of errors. It was the best leg show in town.

Drysdale, whom the Twins routed inside of three innings in the first game, said his old velocity came back to him as the game progressed.

Sam Mele, Minnesota manager, was a bit disturbed that six of Drysdale's eleven strikeouts were called ones. "I don't understand it," Mele said. "They are supposed to take their best cuts, not just stand there."

Drysdale, evening up the Series for his side, said afterwards he changed his book on a number of Minnesota hitters after talking with Claude Osteen, the left-hander who had shut the Twins out the day before.

"Except for a high fastball to Killebrew and a high curve to Oliva, I kept most of my pitches down around the knees. That was all there was to it—just keeping the ball low."

Those two mistakes resulted in home runs. Fortunately for Drysdale and the Dodgers, the bases were bare of runners both times. Those two runs were all the Twins were able to fashion.

With the Series tied up and Koufax scheduled to face the American Leaguers in the fifth game, the Dodgers got back their old strut.

"We have the greatest pitcher in the game going for us," said Drysdale. "I just hope Sandy's on his game. There aren't many times when he's not, believe me. If we win as we should with him, then we go back to Minnesota with two chances to clinch the Series."

"We played some shabby ball," said Mele. "We covered their bunts badly—among other things. Even Roseboro, their catcher, beat one out. How about that? That's cheating a little, isn't it?"

Monday arrived and Koufax didn't disappoint Drysdale, other Dodgers, or the worshipping Angelenos. He shut out Minnesota, with four hits, striking out ten Twins along the way as the Dodgers won their third straight (7-0) after losing the first two games in Minnesota.

The Thursday before when he walked out on the mound to pitch the second game for Los Angeles, everybody expected him to pitch a shutout. He was beaten 5-1, giving up to a pinch-hitter in the seventh inning.

Koufax took his licking like a pro. He admitted to having trouble with his control, but never mentioned the trouble he had adjusting to Metropolitan Stadium's low mound. Instead, he complimented the Minnesota batters.

The baseball men who knew him best advised friends to wait until the next time. They said things would be different.

"I know this sounds kind of silly when you're talking about the best pitcher in the game," said Gene Mauch, the manager of the Phillies, "but I felt sorry for Koufax in that game.

"There he was with about fifty million people watching him at the park and on TV—all expecting nothing less than perfection. Just imagine how he must have felt.

"You know he might have given them a show anyway, but for that catch by Bob Allison. That kept the Dodgers from giving Sandy a run or two. Then he would have had a chance to relax instead of trying to make every pitch perfect.

"I'll bet things will be different the next time he faces them. They're going to be in for a big surprise. He'll be Mr. Koufax the next time."

This time Sandy had a five run lead before Minnesota got a man on base. And when they did, it was because Willie Davis, the centerfielder, misjudged a short fly and let it fall for a short single in the fifth inning. Koufax allowed another scratch hit in the seventh and two legitimate singles in the ninth for a total of four. He walked only one man. Three double-plays rubbed out three of the five base-runners so there were only two left on the bases.

It was the eighty-fourth time he struck out the enemy in double figures. National League clubs withered under his flame thrower eighty-two times when he fanned ten or more, and he set the World Series mark by fanning fifteen Yankees in 1963.

Yet Koufax, always the perfectionist, did not think it was one of his better games. Although he retired twelve batters in a row before Killebrew got his freak hit, Sandy said he never thought about a no-hit, no-run game.

"I didn't think I was throwing that good," he said. "I was surprised they didn't get more hits. My control wasn't sharp and I got awfully tired toward the end.

"I know I only walked one batter but I had too many two-ball, no-strike counts. I had to keep coming back with my fastball when I should have been throwing more curves."

He threw 109 pitches. Seventy per cent of them

BOX SCORE OF 5th SERIES GAME

	AB.	R.	H.	RBI.	PO.	A.
Versalles, ss	4	0	0	0	2	0
Nossek, cf	4	0	1	0	2	0
Oliva, rf	3	0	0	0	2	0
Killebrew, 3b	3	0	1	0	1	1
Battey, c	3	0	0	0	7	1
Allison, lf	2	0	0	0	3	0
Mincher, 1b	3	0	0	0	5	0
Quilici, 2b	3	0	1	0	2	3
Kaat, p	1	0	0	0	0	1
Boswell, p	0	0	0	0	0	0
aRollins	1	0	0	0	0	0
Perry, p	0	0	0	0	0	1
bValdespino	1	0	1	0	0	0
Total	28	0	4	0	24	7

aFlied out for Boswell in 6th.
bSingled for Perry in 9th.

Los Angeles (N.)

	AB.	R.	H.	RBI.	PO.	A.
Wills, ss	5	2	4	1	1	7
Gilliam, 3b	4	1	2	2	0	0
Kennedy, 3b	1	0	0	0	0	0
W. Davis, cf	4	1	2	0	1	0
Johnson, lf	5	1	1	1	2	0
Fairly, rf	5	1	3	1	2	0
Parker, 1b	4	0	0	0	7	0
Tracewski, 2b	3	0	1	0	4	2
Roseboro, c	2	1	0	0	10	0
Koufax, p	4	0	1	1	0	1
Total	37	7	14	6	27	10

Minnesota Twins	0 0 0	0 0 0	0 0 0	–0
Los Angeles Dodgers	2 0 2	1 0 0	2 0 x	–7

Error–Quilici. Double plays–Wills, Tracewski and Parker 2; Wills and Tracewski. Left on bases–Minnesota 2, Los Angeles 11.

Two-base hits–Wills 2, Fairly. Stolen bases–W. Davis 3, Wills. Sacrifces–W. Davis, Parker.

	IP.	H.	R.	ER.	BB.	SO.	HBP.	WP.	BKS.
Kaat (L)	2⅓	6	4	3	0	1	0	0	0
Boswell	2⅔	3	1	1	2	3	0	0	0
Perry	3	5	2	2	1	3	0	0	0
Koufax (W)	9	4	0	0	1	10	0	0	0

Bases on balls–Off Boswell 2 (Tracewski, Roseboro), Perry 1 (Roseboro), Koufax 1 (Allison). Struck out–By Kaat 1 (Koufax), Boswell 3 (Roseboro, Koufax 2), Perry 3 (W. Davis, Tracewski, Parker), Koufax 10 (Killebrew, Allison 2, Quilici, Kaat, Oliva 2, Mincher, Versalles 2).

Umpires–Stewart (A.), plate; Vargo (N.), first base; Hurley (A.), second base; Venzon (N.), third base; Flaherty (A.), left field; Sudol (N.), right field. Time of game–2:34. Attendance–55, 801.

were fastballs, he said, and the rest curves or fork-balls—developed as his change of pace pitch.

Someone mentioned the fact that it was his twenty-eighth complete game of the year.

"That so?", he said. "Then just let's say that maybe I was entitled to get a little tired along about the 350th inning."

The pitcher lauded his teammates, Maury Wills and Willie Davis, for their tremendous playing. Wills took three hits away from the Twins, converting two of the stops into double-plays, and Davis starred at bat and running the bases.

Koufax had long since gotten used to the Dodgers' ping-pong attack. The seven runs he got this time were an unusual luxury. But he said he thought that the fact his team wasn't overburdened with run scorers might be making him a better pitcher.

"The fact that our club doesn't score a lot makes you keep bearing down out there," he said. "You've got to shut 'em out for the first five or six innings. You start your game with the idea of not giving up a run. Until you get those five or six, you've got to assume you're getting only one."

Among the many Minnesotans Koufax impressed was Dr. Bill Proffit, the Twins' physician. "You would never have thought that Koufax could pitch consistently with that arthritis in his elbow," he marveled after watching Sandy.

"At least you'd think he'd have to rest every three or four pitching starts, but he doesn't. The way he pitches has been amazing."

Wills, the speedster who turned the Series into a track meet sat in front of his locker patiently printing the score and a few other details on a baseball.

"It's for Sandy," he said, "but if he doesn't want it for his collection, I'll take it.

"You know I sometimes think it's easier to play behind pitchers like Drysdale and Osteen," he continued. "They let the batters hit the ball. Sandy strikes out so many you sometimes relax too much out there and take a nap."

Now the two teams returned to Minnesota for the sixth game. Sam Mele was as happy as a trailing manager could be about it.

"It comes down to this," he said. "Dodger Stadium is tailor-made for the Dodgers. But I'm convinced they'll have trouble winning in our place."

The Dodgers did have trouble in the Twin's theatre as Mudcat Grant and Jim Katt out-pitched Drysdale and Koufax in the first two games of the tournament.

But once the action moved to the wide-open spaces of the Dodgers' playpen, the Minnesota power was stifled, the Twins earning a lowly team batting average of .157 in three games there.

The Walter Alstons, who fashioned a team average of .245 during the season and hit only seventy-eight home runs (seventy-two fewer than Minnesota) had compiled these marks in the first five games: They made fifty-one hits for a collective batting mark of .302. They also stole nine bases.

The Twins made thirty-three hits for a team batting mark of .213. They stole one base.

Everything bothered the Minnesotans in Los Angeles—the flame-throwing of Koufax, the hard infield that encouraged Dodger bunts and leg hits, the heat, the smog and the way the white shirt sleeves of the customers spoiled the background for the hitters.

Now they were home again and happy and Mudcat

Grant, the laughing extrovert, helped them beat the Dodgers 5-1 with some superlative pitching and a three-run homer to even the series.

Grant, pitching with two days' rest and a nagging cold, allowed six hits. Claude Osteen, his pitching versus, was tagged for a two-run homer by Bob Allison, but the real shocker was the Mudcat's blast into the seats in the sixth.

"I just said to myself I've got to hit the first ball that's a good pitch," he said happily. "And he threw me a good one the first time—a good curve."

Mudcat allowed as how his two Series wins would help the nightclub and hotel tour his musical group planned after the Series.

"It's gonna be called Mudcat and his Kittens," he said. "A guitar, three girls, another fellow and myself. A real cool, swinging group. We'll probably play every place but Dodger Stadium."

Someone asked the Mudcat man if he thought his team could win it now.

"Why not?" he said. "They picked us to finish in the second division before the season even started. Then they said we'd fall apart in September. Then they said those big, bad Dodgers would murder us in the Series. Well, we're still alive. You didn't see Maury Wills or any other Dodger run all over us today."

Alston wasn't sure who would be his pitching choice for the seventh game.

"I've got Drysdale with three days' rest and a bruised pitching hand," he said, "or Koufax with two days' rest.

"I've noticed that left-handers do pretty well getting them out. But whichever one it is I start, the other one will be in the bullpen along with Ron Perranoski."

Both Drysdale and Koufax said they were willing either way.

"It really doesn't make any difference," Sandy told him. "I've already pitched 351 innings this year so a few more won't matter much. My arm in either case is, well—tired."

"It'll be Jim Katt for us," said Sam Mele, "and behind him we'll have everybody ready, even Camilo Pascual."

They debated the identity of the Brooklyn starter long into the early morning hours at press headquarters. The assembled inexperts argued fiercely the pros and cons of Drysdale vis a vis Koufax.

Alston, sitting at a table there, listened for a while then said, "You fellows haven't helped me a bit," and ambled off to bed.

The team had not yet been made aware of Alston's choice as a brief meeting began in the clubhouse the morning of the game. Since it would be their last meeting of the year, the manager expressed his thanks for their play all season long and urged one and all to watch his weight and report back in shape for spring training. Then, quietly he announced:

"Koufax will start."

"It was," he said later, "one of the toughest decisions I ever had to make."

It was the kind of a problem every manager in the major leagues would like to have the pleasure of wrestling with—like trying to decide whether to date Sophia Loren or Brigitte Bardot, whether to buy a castle in Spain or a chalet on the Riviera.

Alston said that he had given the matter deep

thought the night before and that morning. He had to decide how Drysdale, a pitcher who had won twenty-five games for him, a man of great pride, would take it.

He had sounded out both men separately then called them together and told them he hadn't decided.

"We told him that whatever the choice it would be all right with us," Koufax recalls.

The morning of the game he had taken the two aside again and told them it would be Sandy. He also said that Drysdale would be hustled in from the bullpen at the first sign of distress.

Ron Fairly, hearing the manager's quiet announcement of his choice, nodded and asked a visiting journalist:

"When you have the greatest pitcher in baseball on your side, wouldn't you want him pitching the clutch game for you?"

A few hours later Koufax completed a season of stupendous personal accomplishment by pitching the Dodgers to a 2–0 decision over the Twins for the championship of the universe.

Less than seven months before, the twenty-nine-year-old left-hander had started his eleventh season in the major leagues with arthritis throbbing his pitching elbow. He had reason to fear his career might be prematurely finished. One week before the season opened no one, not even members of the medical profession, could tell him whether he would be a once-a-week performer, or even if he would ever pitch again.

Then he went on to win twenty-six games, pitch 360 innings and serve as a losing streak stopper, as the Dodgers rose from sixth place in the National

League to first. All this with an arm that required constant medical attention.

On this big day, pitching with only two days' rest, one fewer than any healthy pitcher usually requires, he overpowered the Twins after a shaky start, burning fastballs past the last two hitters to strike them out.

In an atmosphere of intense drama, he held the Paul Bunyans of the North country to three hits, walked three and struck out his usual ten.

He did all this in a place that seemed as eerie as a Charles Addams spook house. The record crowd of 50,596 made hardly a sound. The funeral flavor was increased by the soft organ music played between innings.

The ushers stood at their posts in the aisles like pall-bearers waiting for services for the deceased to end. The customers did not seem to be in Metropolitan Stadium at all, but rather surrounding the family plot in some cemetery.

With his last pitch, Koufax was too weary to show even his usual elation. He did no handstands, no jig of joy. Even his teammates avoided the customary mob scene in the pitcher's box.

It wasn't, in fact, until he had crossed the foul line on the way to the dugout that the other Dodgers caught up with him. Then his most excited companion was Lou Johnson, the thirty-two-year-old left fielder who, after wandering about the minors for years, had become a Dodger in May only because Tommy Davis had broken an ankle.

It was Johnson's home run off of Jim Kaat in the fourth inning that had provided the margin Koufax needed.

When Alston had called the team meeting at eleven o'clock that morning everybody was there but Johnson.

"There was so much excitement that I purposely missed the bus," he told the boss blandly. "I wanted to get to the ball park real slow an' relaxed."

"You'd even be late for your own funeral," fumed the manager. "From now on when you're late I'm gonna slap a fine on you and another on your body-guard, Willie Davis."

"He's been the most amazing one on this team," said Koufax of Johnson. "When Tommy Davis was hurt we could have folded for sure. But Lou moved in from nowhere. Believe me, no Johnson, no pennant."

The two-run lead they gave Sandy in the fourth was not so big that Alston could take risks. He had Drysdale up and down in the bullpen, warming up in every odd-numbered inning from the first to the ninth.

Sandy wasn't as true on target as he customarily is, although he did strike out ten. He was, rather, just as good as he had to be, and that's the mark of a real pitcher.

By the time the meatier portion of the Minnesota lineup came up in the ninth, the big snap had gone out of his curveball and he seemed tired.

Jim Gilliam, the thirty-seven-year-old coach who had come out of retirement to play 111 games at third base, had made a sensational backhanded stop to protect Sandy's 2–0 lead in the fifth, now sat watching and fretting before the television set in the Los Angeles clubhouse. John Kennedy had replaced him at third base.

"He's pitching on instinct now," Gilliam said, "pure instinct."

Once again when the game was over, Sandy said he felt, "tired and thrilled and a hundred years old. My control wasn't good," he admitted, "and I had no real curve most of the time.

"I lost my rhythm some in the fifth when I reared back too far and tried to put too much on the ball. That's when the skipper came out and told me to cut down, to just use my regular energy to pitch. After that, I was all right.

"Overall, I don't think I pitched quite as well today as I did on Monday in Los Angeles. I had a better curve then. Today I stuck pretty much to my fastball. My arm never got sore, but just to make sure I had some hot stuff rubbed on it after the fifth inning."

He allowed only three hits. Versalles hit a curve and Quilici and Killebrew hit fastballs.

"That relief pitching isn't for me," whined Drysdale afterward. "I was up and down like a yo-yo out there. I got cross-eyed just looking through that chicken wire."

Someone asked Drysdale to name the better pitcher.

"We're different types," he answered. "He's left-handed, I'm right-handed."

"If I had my choice, I think I'd always go with a left-hander against Minnesota," said Alston, "But I tell you it wasn't an easy choice."

"I guess Sandy and I put the skipper on the spot by our attitude," Drysdale said. "Maybe we should have had one helluva fight in there."

But there wasn't, of course, any chance of a fight.

The two pitchers are very close and appreciative of each other's great skills.

"I couldn't think of anybody I'd rather bring in as a relief pitcher than Drysdale," said Alston. "And if I started Koufax I'd still have Drysdale available as a pinch-hitter as well as a relief pitcher. Also Drysdale warms up faster in the bullpen than Koufax.

"Another thing—with Ron Perranoski in the bullpen, I could set up a Koufax-Drysdale-Perranoski sequence, left, right, left."

The happy, excited chatter in the clubhouse continued as the players moved about, champagne spilling from their paper cups. Some poured the festive liquid over their teammates' heads. A few non-comformists drank the poor man's bubbly—beer.

Jim Gilliam was replaying the diving stab he made of Versalles' third base drive that could have ignited a Minnesota rally in the fifth; there had been runners on first and second, with one out.

The 50,596 customers may have sighed like a huge, pricked balloon, but Koufax appreciated the great play.

"If Jim doesn't come up with that ball," Sandy had told himself, "then I don't finish the game."

"I was playing Versalles on the line," said Gilliam. "I knew Sandy didn't have his best stuff. When I knew a curve ball was coming I protected the line. The ball was hit, I reacted."

"It was the key play for us," agreed Alston. "No, I'm not going to say that Koufax was one pitch away from leaving the game but we had some good pitchers ready in the bullpen."

Koufax said that before he left for a Hawaiian vacation, he would undergo a thorough examination of

BOX SCORE OF 7th SERIES GAME

Los Angeles (N.)	AB.	R.	H.	RBI.	PO.	A.
Wills, ss	4	0	0	0	2	4
Gilliam, 3b	5	0	2	0	2	1
Kennedy, 3b	0	0	0	0	0	1
W. Davis, cf	2	0	0	0	1	0
Johnson, lf	4	1	1	1	3	0
Fairly, rf	4	1	1	0	0	0
Parker, 1b	4	0	2	1	6	0
Tracewski, 2b	4	0	0	0	1	0
Roseboro, c	2	0	1	0	12	0
Koufax, p	3	0	0	0	0	1
Total	32	2	7	2	27	7

Minnesota (A.)	AB.	R.	H.	RBI.	PO.	A.
Versalles, ss	4	0	1	0	0	2
Nossek, cf	4	0	0	0	0	0
Oliva, rf	3	0	0	0	4	0
Killebrew, 3b	3	0	1	0	2	2
Battey, c	4	0	0	0	8	1
Allison, lf	4	0	0	0	1	0
Mincher, 1b	3	0	0	0	10	0
Quilici, 2b	3	0	1	0	1	3
Kaat, p	1	0	0	0	0	1
Worthington, p	0	0	0	0	1	1
aRollins	0	0	0	0	0	0
Klippstein, p	0	0	0	0	0	0
Merritt, p	0	0	0	0	0	0
bValdespino	1	0	0	0	0	0
Perry, p	0	0	0	0	0	0
Total	30	0	3	0	27	10

aWalked for Worthington in 5th.
bFouled out for Merrit in 8th.

Los Angeles Dodgers	0 0 0	2 0 0	0 0 0	–2
Minnesota Twins	0 0 0	0 0 0	0 0 0	–0

Error–Oliva. Left on bases–Los Angeles 9, Minnesota 6.

Two-base hits–Roseboro, Fairly, Quilici. Three-base hit–Parker. Home run–Johnson. Sacrifice–W. Davis.

	IP.	H.	R.	ER.	BB.	SO.	HBP.	WP.	BKS.
Koufax (W)	9	3	0	0	3	10	0	0	0
Kaat (L)	3	5	2	2	1	2	0	0	0
Worthington	2	0	0	0	1	0	0	0	0
Klippstein	1⅔	2	0	0	1	2	1	0	0
Merritt	1⅓	0	0	0	0	1	0	0	0
Perry	1	0	0	0	1	1	0	0	0

Faced 3 batters in 4th.

Bases on balls–Off Koufax 3 (Oliva, Killebrew, Rollins), Kaat 1 (Koufax), Worthington 1 (Roseboro) 1, Klippstein 1 (Roseboro), Perry (Wills). Struck out–By Koufax 10 (Versalles, Battey 2, Allison 2, Mincher, Kaat, Oliva 2, Quilici), Kaat 2 (Wills, Tracewski, Klippstein 2 (Tracewski, Koufax), Merritt 1 (Roseboro), Perry 1 (Koufax). Hit by pitcher–By Klippstein (W. Davis).

Umpires–Hurley (A.), plate; Venzon (N.), first base; Flaherty (A.), second base; Sudol (N.), third base; Stewart (A.), left field; Vargo (N.), right field. Time of game–2:27. Attendance–50,596.

his left arm, which he was forced to put in the deep freeze for at least half an hour after every game.

"Right now it feels fine. The fact that I know I won't have to use it for the next four and a half months makes it feel even better."

In the losers' clubhouse, Sam Mele agreed that Gilliam's stop of Versalles' drive was the turning point of the game.

"It meant one run for sure and a good chance to score another," said the manager. "Maybe we could have gotten two and tied it up, depending on how the ball caromed off the fence. It was a tremendous play. There's no doubt about it.

"Koufax is a great pitcher," he continued. "He's got tremendous stuff and knows what to do with it. He's the best I've ever seen."

CHAPTER TEN

A CROWD ESTIMATED at 6,000 and ranging in years from babies in arms to eighty-year-olds jammed the American Airlines Terminal in Los Angeles to pay wild tribute to the Dodgers on their return home with the booty.

"We want Sandy! We want Sandy!" they yelled in unison, watching for the Brooklyn boy who had only come into his own after the Dodgers left Brooklyn.

But one, with the voice of a foghorn, put it best: "We want Superarm! We want Superarm!"

In Hollywood, friends were said to be readying a special Oscar for presentation with due hoopla to the world's most famous arthritic case.

The marquee sign over the entrance of the Hyatt House in Los Angeles read:

BLESSED EVENT. SANDY HAS TWINS.

Soon the nation's baseball journalists confirmed what National League players and the Minnesota Twins had known for some time—that southpaw Sandy was the best pitcher in baseball.

After reviewing the year, the writers announced

that they had unanimously picked Koufax to become the first man to win the Cy Young Award twice.

Informed of the honor, the pitcher said it was a wonderful climax to "the most gratifying season I've ever had. It was particularly satisfying this year to win it in a league that has so many great pitchers," he said. "It was a pitcher's year."

Koufax broke all precedent in 1963 being named unanimous choice for the Young Award after a 25–5 record. He also captured the National League's Most Valuable Player Award that season.

The announcement pinpointed the fact that Koufax had led both major leagues in four categories and established two records enroute to his selection.

His twenty-six wins, 336 innings pitched, 382 strikeouts and 2.04 earned-run average were the best among the regular starters in either league.

The citation reminded one and all that his strikeout total broke Rapid Robert Feller's nineteen-year-old single season mark of 348 and that the perfect game he pitched against the Chicago Cubs was his fourth no-hit, no-run job, another modern-day major league record.

Retiring Baseball Commissioner Ford Christopher Frick, said Sandy's selection was "simply great.

"The way Sandy has pitched the last few years his name belongs right there with Cy Young as one of the truly great pitchers of all time," said Frick.

The latest Koufax award gave the Dodger establishment four Cy Young trophies in the ten years of its existence. The winners:

1956–Don Newcombe, Brooklyn Dodgers
1957–Warren Spahn, Milwaukee Braves
1958–Bob Turley, New York Yankees

1959–Early Wynn, Chicago White Sox
1960–Vernon Law, Pittsburgh Pirates
1961–Whitey Ford, New York Yankees
1962–Don Drysdale, Los Angeles Dodgers
1963–Sandy Koufax, Los Angeles Dodgers
1964–Dean Chance, Los Angeles Angels
1965–Sandy Koufax, Los Angeles Dodgers

Soon came announcements of other honors to be bestowed upon the Dodger dandy in banquet halls stretching from Toronto to Monterey, from San Diego to New York. It turned out to be his busiest social, chow and speech-making season since he set records for such engagements after his two devastating jobs on the New York Yankees in the 1963 World Series.

Soon Sandy, who had begged out of an affair to which Milton Berle invited him not so many seasons back because he didn't own a tuxedo, would be suiting up in a tux night after night.

On with the midnight-blue dinner jacket and pantaloons, the dark red cumberbund, the starched white shirt and black bow tie. Off with proud banquet committee members to the festal boards.

There at the head table, in the guest of honor spot, he would again be confronted by the usual rubber chicken, petrified peas, and cement potatoes. Later the chairman would rise, tell a stale story or two, then–

"And now, I give you, a man who . . . Sandy Koufax!"

George Herman (Babe) Ruth set what is believed to be the record for winter banquet commandos when he appeared at 146 such affairs after hitting sixty home runs for the Yankees in 1927.

In 1961 the Yankees' Roger Maris hit sixty-one homers and this, naturally, called for another grand tour of the banquet circuit. Roger, however, reminded that Ruth had once waddled into spring training camp forty-eight pounds overweight because of his free-style banqueting, cut his schedule. He finished far short of the pace set by the Babe.

Koufax too, fell way short of the Babe's gastronomic tour record, which was one of the reasons Sandy was able to win nineteen games for the Dodgers in 1964.

Nevertheless, Sandy's schedule began to look formidable as early as November.

Murray Goodman announced that the prize pitcher would head a special railroad convoy to Rochester, New York, where, on January 23, he would again receive the $10,000 Hickok Belt as the Professional Athlete of the Year. It would make him the trophy's first two-time winner since they also wrapped it around him in 1963.

Then came notice from Jim Hearn, the old Giant pitcher, and Jerry Coleman, the former Yankee infielder, that Koo would be summoned to the Royal Box of the Hotel Americana in New York to get the Van Heusen Outstanding Achievement Award. Here too Sandy repeated, since they also named him in 1963.

On top of that, the news that he had been named to receive both the Sid Mercer Memorial (Player of the Year) and Babe Ruth (World Series star) Awards by the New York Chapter of the Baseball Writers' Association, at their forty-second annual clambake at the Americana, January 30.

It was the second time Koufax had been voted

both the Mercer and Ruth Awards in the same season. He had previously won them in 1964.

He was the first player ever to repeat as the Ruth winner and only Joe DiMaggio (1938 and 1942), Ted Williams (1943 and 1958) and Mickey Mantle (1957 and 1961) repeated as Mercer winners since the award was first presented in 1931.

In early January Sandy's Studio City, California, postman delivered a letter with a Dodger letterhead on the envelope to the Koufax mail-drop. Sandy knew what it was before he even opened it—his 1966 contract.

He also knew that the figures it contained meant nothing, that it was a token thing, because baseball contracts had to go out to the players before January 15. This one could mention the same salary as the previous.

Serious discussion of how much he was worth to the Dodgers would come later, when he and Buzzy Bavasi sat down eyeball to eyeball. Sandy said he didn't expect any trouble.

Before the World Series ended everyone agreed that the Dodger demi-god would get a contract calling for $100,000-plus, maybe enough to pass Willie Mays' salary. It would make Koufax the highest paid player on the planet.

High-money man among the pitchers before Koufax arrived, was Bob Feller, who was paid $93,000 one season by the Cleveland Indians. Feller had a bonus arrangement with the club, however, based on attendance; his base pay was around $46,000.

Some advised Koufax to go for a bonus-type contract with the Dodgers, because he was now at his peak as a gate attraction.

There was an advance ticket window at Dodger Stadium known as the Koufax line. People lined up in front of it days ahead of time figuring the date on which he would work and—who knows?—pitch another no-hitter.

The Dodgers themselves estimated during the 1965 season that Koufax's advertised presence in the box meant 10,000 extra customers at the gate. On the road he was regarded as worth 15,000 extra. At Shea Stadium in New York, it meant a sellout or thereabouts no matter how the Mets were doing.

There always was a bum rap on Walter Alston, one of the men who had much to do with making Koufax the magnificent pitching machine and meal-ticket he is today.

He had no color, it went. He was dull. He never said anything.

"Yeah," said someone, tired of listening, "all he does is win pennants."

Sandy at work rarely shows emotion. Errors do not bother him, or cause him to scuff the mound with his toe in indignation. Umpires like to work his games because, among other things, he doesn't complain about their judgement. The fans never get under his skin. But there were times. . . .

Once, at Wrigley Field in Chicago during one of his formative seasons, Sandy was getting a pretty good lathering from the Cub hitters. He was also getting a pretty good going-over from the fans, particularly those behind the Dodger dugout.

Finally it became necessary to take him out of the box. Sandy strode angrily for the dugout as the jeers increased. Just before he got there, he stopped, lifted his cap, and gave his hecklers a mock bow.

Afterwards Alston took him aside.

"You shouldn't have done that," said the manager. "It's bush. It didn't accomplish anything and it spoiled the image you've been building up. Don't do it again."

Then there was that early spring at Vero Beach. Sandy and a roommate, who had been having a late snack after a movie out of town, came in after the curfew hour and Alston saw them.

The pair saw the manager at the same time and a journalist there reported a musical comedy chase around and through the barracks. Koufax and his roomie finally made it and locked their door.

Alston, storming up a minute later, rained angry blows upon the woodwork with his fists.

"Why didn't you kick it instead?" someone asked the next day.

"Because," replied Walter, "I didn't have my shoes on."

Alston, a quiet, modest reflective man, was only in his sophomore year as manager of the Dodgers when the Koufax bonus baby was dropped into his lap. Known for his astute handling of pitchers, he stayed with Sandy through those long, wild, losing years.

One wonders how the young pitcher would have fared had either Leo Durocher or Charley Dressen, his predecessors, been in charge.

Leo, at first sight of Sandy's blinding speed would undoubtedly have exclaimed: "He's a pistol, he's my boy!" The vitriolic-tongued Durocher might not have held still, however, for Koufax's early years, no matter what the front office said.

Dressen would have been moved to exuberant quotes too after watching Sandy for the first time. Charley, who could see a twenty-game winner in the greenest of rookies, would probably have predicted that and more for the Koufax kid, but it probably wouldn't be long before he would have sought to change the young man's motion.

Koufax, nevertheless, will be nicely represented by one some day in baseball's hallowed Hall of Fame in Cooperstown, New York.

There, in a large glass case, will be the figure of Sandy Koufax in a Dodger uniform, his left arm halted in the act of firing a baseball through the glass, the room and the red brick wall.

A big brass plate at the foot of the shrine will attest to the many outstanding achievements that not only got him in the front door but to a favored spot front and center with Babe Ruth, Cy Young, Casey Stengel, Honus Wagner, Walter Johnson, Christy Mathewson and other paid-up members.

The plate will note that the fine figure of a fellow above had guaranteed his immortality by, among others, the following achievements:

- Struck out eighteen batters in a game twice, breaking Dizzy Dean's National League record of seventeen and equaling Bob Feller's major league record. (Feller accomplished it only once);
- Struck out fifteen batters in a World Series game, breaking Carl Erskine's mark of fourteen;

• Pitched four no-hit, no-run games, more than any man in baseball history;

• Struck out 382 men in 1965, breaking his own record of 306 set in 1963;

• Led the National League in earned runs average four years in succession (1962, 1963, 1964, 1965), breaking the record set by Grover Cleveland Alexander in 1914, 1915, and 1916;

• Struck out the most men in a night game (18);

• Pitched eleven shutouts in 1963, setting a National League record for left-handers;

• Struck out ten or more batters eighty-two times, breaking the record of fifty-four shared by Bob Feller and Rube Waddell;

• Struck out the most men in two consecutive nine-inning games (31);

• Struck out 200 or more batters for five consecutive seasons (1961, 1962, 1963, 1964, 1965).

Among the marks left for Sandy Koufax to aim at were:

• Most innings pitched (384 by Rube Waddell in 1904);

• Most innings pitched in the National League (347 by Robin Roberts of the Philadelphia Phillies);

• Most years leading earned-run average (nine by Robert M. Grove of the Philadelphia Athletics and Boston Red Sox);

• Most years leading earned run average in the National League (five by Grover Cleveland Alexander of the Philadelphia Phillies);

• A thirty-win season (last achieved by Dizzy Dean of the St. Louis Cardinals in 1934).

The view from the top was splendid, but Koufax must have often thought of how much more magnificent it might have been if it had not been for all those wasted years.

A couple of seasons work in the minor leagues might have solved his control problem early and enabled him to win big in the National League three, four or five years before he found himself.

At the end of 1960, after six seasons in Dodger suiting, he could look back on a grand total of thirty-six wins against forty defeats.

By contrast Warren Spahn, who started the 1964 season with 356 victories in the bank, had won 108 games at the end of his sixth season with the then Boston Braves.

Walter Johnson, also in the same 300-or-more-wins division, gained 416 wins in his twenty-one-year career, and got 114 of them in his first six years. Lefty Grove, with a 300 lifetime total, won 115. To go back even further, Cy Young, who won 511 during his twenty-two-year career, accounted for 164 of them in his first six years with Cleveland.

It is a fair assumption that if Koufax had had the needed minor league experience in 1955 and 1956, he would have won more than the thirty-two games he accounted for in 1957, 1958, 1959 and 1960.

Koufax had a career bundle of 138 wins at the close of the 1965 season, with a goal of 300-plus, his arthritic elbow willing.

"It takes a lot of things to win 300 or more games," says Warren Spahn today, "but the big thing is in being able to pitch long enough to get that many.

"Sandy has the tools—that great fastball and just as great a curve. He'll probably get even better than he is right now.

"If he isn't hurt he'll probably be able to throw that great fast one for another six, seven or eight years. After that he's got to develop new pitches to compensate for his loss of speed.

"I developed my screwball in 1954, then afterward I managed to add a slider. I had lost a lot off my fastball but those extra pitches more than made up for that. They couldn't lay for the fast one. The fact that I never had arm trouble of any sort and that my legs stayed good also helped me last so long. I was lucky.

Koufax had something in common with Johnson, the famed fireballer of the Washington Senators from 1907 to 1927.

"He was the only pitcher," Bill Evans, a great umpire once confessed, "who threw so hard I couldn't steel myself against closing my eyes whenever the ball came whistling toward the plate.")

Like Johnson, Sandy had to put up with a team that often found the manufacture of runs one of the mysteries of life. Walter spent a lifetime with a Washington club that could do little to help its pitchers and usually wound up in the second division.

When the Dodgers had their powerhouse clubs and hitsmiths like Roy Campanella, Carl Furillo, Gil Hodges, Jackie Robinson, Duke Snider, Pee Wee Reese and others, Sandy was just growing up as a pitcher. At any rate, he wasn't able to benefit from their bats as a regular starter.

From 1961 to and including the 1965 season, they

could boast of only five operatives able to hit .300 or better and one of them was Don Drysdale, their only .300 hitter in 1965.

To win the pennant they had to scrounge for runs like bums in a trash bin. Their offensive often consisted of a bunt, a pass and a prayer. They had to steal bases—and ball games.

Their team batting average was only .245, lowest ever for a pennant winner and something they kept quiet about, like a skeleton in the closet. There were probably heavier hitting teams in the Little League. Seldom have so many hit so few.

Grove, in his salad seasons, had Al Simmons, Mickey Cochrane, Jimmy Foxx, Jimmy Dykes and other muscular members of Connie Mack's good Philadelphia teams fashioning runs for him.

Dean, in his thirty win season and other big ones, had the substantial backing of such Gashouse Gangsters as Frankie Frisch, Pepper Martin, Joe Medwick, Terry Moore, Rip Collins, Don Gutteridge, Johnny Mize and others.

Koufax would undoubtedly have set even more amazing records in 1963, 1964 and 1965 had he been backed by the offensive support of a team like Cincinnati. The Reds led the National League in hitting in 1965 with a .273 average and runs scored with 825. They hit 183 homers.

When Koufax first began firing his high hard one past big league batters in earnest they asked if he were faster than Bob Feller and other human howitzers. After Sandy's record 382 strikeouts in 1965 they asked who is faster than Koufax.

The answer could be, "nobody, past or present." The fellow could have superior strikeout skill to

Feller, Johnson, Vance, Grove, Waddell and Marquard.

There was a hint which you could not find in the records. He was the only pitcher the figure filberts could uncover down through the years, who averaged better than a strikeout per inning for more than 200 innings. It was 382 in 335⅔ innings in 1965.

Most pitchers get smart and learn to pace themselves, applying the mustard only when needed, but that savvy doesn't come in a hurry. Most strikeout feats occur in a pitcher's early years.

Herb Score led the American League with 244 in 227 innings as a rookie. Mathematicians, putting it on a per-game basis, said his pace was 9.68 for every nine innings in 1946.

Hal Newhouser registered 8.45 and Feller 8.44 in 1941, Rube Marquard 7.74 in 1911, Dazzy Vance 7.63 in 1924, Walter Johnson 7.52 in 1910 and Christy Mathewson 6.55 in 1903.

Name all the great pitchers of the past—Christy Mathewson, Cy Young, Lefty Grove, Walter Johnson, Grover Cleveland Alexander, Bob Feller, Warren Spahn, Dizzy Dean, and check their records and you couldn't find one who put together as great a season as Koufax did in 1965.

Here are the best seasons of four of them, compared with Sandy's splendid season:

	G	IP	H	BB	SO	W	L	ERA
Walter Johnson (1913) ...	48	346	232	38	243	36	7	1.14
Dizzy Dean (1934)	50	312	288	75	195	30	7	2.62
Warren Spahn (1953)	35	266	211	70	148	23	7	2.10
Bob Feller (1946)	48	371	135	41	222	17	3	2.18
Sandy Koufax (1965)	43	333 2/3	216	71	382	26	8	2.04

They wondered out loud what was Koufax's proper place. The old gaffers said to wait a while before trying to rate him.

The 1965 season was Sandy's eleventh. In that oldsters agreed, but quite a few less than Cy Young's 511, Walter Johnson's 414, Kid Nicol's 364 or Warren Spahn's 356.

Nicol's fifteen year career extended six years into the modern era before he retired in 1906. Mathewson called him the greatest pitcher he ever saw.

To attain the marks and years of service of the immortals, Sandy's arthritic left elbow must be as willing and able as it was in winning twenty-six games.

"There's absolutely no guarantee, of course, that it will be that good again," said Dr. Kerlan, the Dodgers' physician, himself bent from rheumatoid arthritis in his back.

"Sandy surprised me wonderfully last season and I hope he does so again. But at the same time I wouldn't have been one bit surprised last season if, instead, he had been forced to stop pitching for some extended periods. Instead he didn't miss one turn. But it could happen, it could flare up on him any time."

As long as he continues to pitch, Koufax will have to spend extra time on the rubbing table, getting special back rubs and arm-stretching exercises, not to mention a number of gooey applications of red hot Capsolin Ointment, which brings the blood to the surface.

More treatment comes after a game and includes the twenty minute ice bath for the afflicted elbow.

When he first came back from spring training with arthritis, the doctors first had to drain the elbow and inject anti-inflammatory material directly into the joint. For a while this had to be done constantly.

Later Dr. Kerlan worked out a pill schedule for the pitcher. This called for his taking capsules containing butazolidin alka, an anti-inflammatory agent, after breakfast the day before he pitched, the day of the game and the day after.

"Sandy Koufax took beautiful Jill St. John to Milton Berle's big Flamingo opening in Las Vegas," reported Earl Wilson's column in the New York *Post.*

Lines like that, coupling him with various stars and starlets have appeared in the papers ever since Koufax made it big with the Dodgers.

After all, the guy is good-looking, a bachelor, and a big name.

To one gushy Hollywood columnist he is Cary Grant, Rock Hudson and Sean Connery rolled into one. All a press agent has to do to get the name of one of his lady clients into this one's daily column is to link her name to Sandy's.

If he had actually escorted all the women this particular dot-and-dasher has had Koufax taking to swank eating places, night clubs or affairs, the fellow wouldn't have had time to win one ball game, let alone twenty-six.

To his Los Angeles teammates he is a class guy. A bit of a loner who moves about mostly by himself, perhaps, but a guy who is good company when he's around the team.

"Outside the ball park we don't see much of him when we're on the road," reports one teammate. He eats out a lot. If we do bump into him around town, he may be with a doll. If so, you can bet that she's good-looking."

The adulation that pours over Koufax in the ball park doesn't end with the ball game. He'd like to be just another ball player but the ladies, young and old, won't let him.

Coming out of the park he has to move through mobs of squealing, screaming admirers, much in the fashion of a headlined rock and roll singer, before he reaches his bronze Oldsmobile. ("He uses his Olds for trips to the ball park and to stand on when he washes his Rolls Royce," runs a Dodger clubhouse gag.)

Not even Walter Alston, who gets a lot of written advice every day on how to run the ball club, where to put this player or that in the batting order, who to pitch and when, gets more mail than Sandy.

At Dodger Stadium he averages four dozen letters a day from all over the country, much of it in feminine handwriting and smelling like a garden in spring.

> Gentleman, began a letter to the Dodgers after Sandy had injured his shoulder in 1963, It distresses me to hear of Sandy's injury, but maybe I can be of some service. I am a registered masseuse, a graduate of a Swedish physical therapy school and would dearly love to rub him.
>
> Yours sincerely, Lillian ————

To protect him from pests on the road, the club often registers him in a room he never uses.

Then Sandy actually rooms, unregistered, with

Dick Tracewski, the infielder. The latter screens all phone calls or other attempts to get through to the pitcher by people who learn of the rooming arrangement.

Tracewski and his more famous roomie often kill the boring hours on road trips listening to the portable radio and tape recorder Sandy almost always carries with him. Leo Durocher used to kid him about being a walking music box.

At home Koufax lives the good life but makes it an unspectacular one and as private as possible. He is discriminating in his choice of friends and places.

Because he knows kids could be easily influenced by what he does, he refuses to endorse cigarette advertising.

There were so many exaggerations of the young man's bachelor way of life told and written since he began to capture the public's imagination that they became a source of merriment and annoyance to Koufax.

He bought a modest $40,000 ranch-type house that sits on a knoll on a half-acre plot in a lonely section of the San Fernando Valley near Los Angeles. Soon he was reading that he lived in a huge Hollywood mansion with more than a dozen rooms.

Actually his tastefully furnished house consists of two bed rooms, a den, a kitchen and a living room. There is a two-car garage and swimming pool. An elderly housekeeper takes care of the place.

He makes his own breakfast; other meals he eats out. On the day he is to pitch, his breakfast often consists of a steak as well as eggs.

"I only have two meals the day I pitch," he explained, "and the first one has to carry me until I can have a sandwich after the game."

For a number of years sportwriters and baseball fans who did not know him thought Sandy was an aloof, somewhat stuffy young fellow who, like Garbo, wanted to be alone.

The truth of the matter was that he was merely shy, like a small boy getting up before his class to make his first public recitation.

Sandy used to seem somewhat terrified when, after some particularly great game, the reporters and photographers rushed to his locker in the Dodger clubhouse.

In more recent seasons he's grown more accustomed to the big hurrah that so often surrounds him. He answers most questions no matter how silly or how often repeated, and he's an ever-willing radio and TV subject.

He undoubtedly feels the pressure at times and would probably rather pitch to Versalles, Oliva, Killebrew, Battey and other Minnesota Twins all over again than to submit to another interview or pose for "just one more" picture. It has never made him unpleasant, however, or brought about any hassles with the press.

Regularly they ask Sandy if he has any matrimonial plans.

"The man who is called baseball's most eligible bachelor says he will get married "when I meet the right girl." So wrote Judy Michaelson in the *New York Post*, calling him discreet and discriminating. One of his girl friends was runner-up in a big beauty contest.

To Walter Alston, the mid-Western rustic who is

his boss, Sandy is a quiet type, easy to handle. "But he's like a lot of ball players in one respect, he can be quite a needler."

Meanwhile mothers all over America, hearing and reading about this prosperous, handsome, thirty-year-old bachelor, often think of what a beautiful catch he would make for their daughter.

Wouldn't it be something, they daydream, in talking to friends and neighbors, to toss off a casual reference to:

"My son-in-law, the baseball pitcher. . . ."

Pitching Record
Koufax, Sanford (Sandy)

Bats right. Throws left. Height 6 feet, 2 inches, Weight 205 lbs.

	Club	G	IP	W	L	PCT.	GS	CG	SHO
1955	Brooklyn	12	42	2	2	.500	5	2	2
1956	Brooklyn	16	59	2	4	.333	10	0	0
1957	Brooklyn	34	104	5	4	.556	13	2	0
1958	L.A.	40	159	11	11	.500	26	5	0
1959	L.A.	35	153	8	6	.571	23	6	1
1960	L.A.	37	175	8	13	.381	26	7	2
1961	L.A.	42	256	18	13	.581	35	15	2
1962	L.A.	28	184	14	7	.667	26	11	2
1963	L.A.	40	311	25	5	.833	40	20	11
1964	L.A.	29	233	19	5	.792	28	15	7
1965	L.A.	43	333 2/3	26	8	.765	41	27	8
Major totals (11 yrs.)		356	2001 2/3	138	78	.565	273	110	35

Pitching Record (con't)

YEAR	R	H	HRS	BB	SO	BKS	WP	BB	ERA
1955	15	33	2	28	30	0	0	1	3.00
1956	37	66	10	29	30	2	1	0	4.88
1957	49	83	14	51	122	0	5	2	3.89
1958	89	132	19	105	131	0	17	1	4.47
1959	74	136	23	92	173	1	5	0	4.06
1960	83	133	20	100	197	0	9	1	3.91
1961	117	212	27	96	269	2	12	3	3.52
1962	61	134	13	57	216	0	3	2	2.54
1963	68	214	18	58	306	1	6	3	1.88
1964	49	154	13	53	223	0	9	0	1.74
1965	90	216	25	71	382	0	11	5	2.04
Totals		1533	181	740	2079	6	78	18	3.14

World Series Totals

	Versus	G	IP	W	L	PCT.	GS	CG	SHO
1959	Chicago	2	9	0	1	.000	1	0	0
1963	N.Y.	2	18	2	0	1.000	2	2	0
1965	Minn.	3	24	2	1	.677	3	2	2

World Series Record

	Versus	R	H	HRS	BB	SO	BKS	WP	HB	ERA
1959	Chi.	1	5	0	1	7	0	0	0	0.00
1963	N.Y.	3	12	2	3	23	0	0	0	1.50
1965	Minn.	2	13	0	5	29	0	0	0	0.37

Batting Record

Year	AB	R	H	2B	3B	HR	RBI	PCT.
1955	12	0	0	0	0	0	0	.000
1956	17	0	2	0	0	0	0	.118
1957	26	1	0	0	0	0	0	.000
1958	49	2	6	1	0	0	1	.122
1959	54	3	6	3	0	0	0	.111
1960	57	1	7	0	0	0	1	.123
1961	77	3	5	0	0	0	2	.065
1962	69	1	6	0	0	1	4	.087
1963	110	3	7	0	0	1	7	.064
1964	110	3	7	0	0	0	1	.173
1965	113	4	20	2	0	0	7	.177

EPILOGUE

When the Dodgers assembled at Vero Beach for their first rehearsal for the new season on February 27, 1966, Koufax and Drysdale were prominent by their absence. Taking dead aim at Walter O'Malley's big, fat bankroll, they were demanding a nice round $1 million dollar contract to be split between them over a three-year period.

At first some suspected a publicity stunt. Buzzy Bavasi, the general manager, had sent contracts to the two pitchers and they had sent the contracts back.

"How far apart are you?" someone asked Bavasi.

"About half a million dollars and two years," he replied. He explained that, like other clubs, the Dodgers were opposed to long-term contracts, package deals and, yes, $165,000-per-year players.

"I wish the boys well," said O'Malley. "They're entitled to try and get all they can from Bavasi. But it's another thing when Bavasi tries to get the money from me."

In Los Angeles Koufax said that he and Drysdale and their agent and attorney, Bill Hayes, had put together the package based on what they considered their value to the club.

It was obviously a well thought out plan. There is strength in numbers—and the numbers in this case totaled 49 victories and the extra customers attracted when they pitched.

Statistics showed that every time Drysdale pitched in Chavez Ravine the Dodgers drew some 3,000 more fans than when anybody but Koufax pitched. When Sandy worked they drew 8,000 more. In addition figure filberts claimed that each customer spent an average $4.50 in admission, parking fees and refreshments. Thus, they said, Drysdale put an extra $13,000 in the till each time he started and Koufax kicked in $36,000 every time he pitched.

Two weeks went by. There was a rumor that the pitchers had lowered their price to $375,000 apiece for three years but Bavasi said he hadn't heard from them at all.

"The last I heard they said they weren't impressed by our offer," said Bavasi. His offer was believed somewhere around $100,000 for Koufax and $10,000 less for Drysdale—on one-year papers.

"I wouldn't think of a long-term contract for a pitcher," he said. "Not, anyway, at their age." Koufax was 30 in December, Drysdale was to become 30 in July. And Sandy had a history of arm trouble.

Worse, though, to the man holding the club line, was the idea of two players negotiating together. The other owners, whatever their disputes with O'Malley in the past, were a solid cheering section behind him now. A three-year joint one-million-dollar contract would set a chilling precedent.

"If Koufax wants to give Drysdale some of his money that's all right with me," said Bavazi. "But they shouldn't hold us up. Let Sandy take the money for Drysdale out of his own pocket, not the club's."

Meanwhile back in Los Angeles, it was announced that the two pitchers had signed to make a movie, "Warning Shot," starring David Jansen, for Paramount Studios. A spokesman said work on the film would start April 4, and that it would take at least two weeks for them to complete their roles.

"They will have speaking parts," the spokesman said. "Drysdale will play a television commentator and Koufax a detective sergeant."

"They'll be sensational," said Chuck Connors, the TV cowhand and a former non-curveball hitting first baseman for the Brooklyn Dodgers and Chicago Cubs.

"They're hot properties," said director Buzz Kulik, who envisioned long lines outside movie houses showing what had been originally scheduled as a Grade Z hooker, when the cast included Koufax and Drysdale.

At the same time agent Hayes said that Henry Saperstein and Ruben Burkovich, U.S. representatives for Toho, a Japanese theatrical syndicate, were working on a tour of Japan for the baseball stars. He said the junket would take from 30 to 60 days and earn the pair "six figure" salaries.

About this time O'Malley piously intoned, "Well, as they leave baseball, I wish them well. They are entitled to go out of the game with the greatest dignity."

The man meant that he had made his final offer but it seems it wasn't that at all. A few hours later

Koufax and Drysdale, the pot sweetened again by O'Malley's agent, Bavasi, called off their holdout.

They abandoned their demand for a three-year contract for both, or the one-third million dollars yearly they asked in a package deal. But they signed as an entry for an estimated $220,000. They wouldn't say how they would split it, but most seemed to agree that Koo's salary would exceed $115,000 and Don's would be about $105,000. They had held out for 32 days.

Drysdale revealed that he and Sandy had a legal curve ready to throw at the club if they failed to come to terms. They were prepared to file suit through their attorney under a so-called "anti-slavery law."

"It's the personal services contract code," he explained. "Under California law it provides that a company, such as a studio, cannot keep anyone under contract for more than seven years.

"Even if both sides want to continue the contract, it still has to be terminated and a new one drawn up. This is to prevent—well, as they say—to prevent slavery."

Koufax had been under Dodger contract since 1955 and Drysdale since 1956.

Drysdale said the act had been invoked in 1944 when actress Olivia DeHavilland broke her movie contract.

It says here that Koufax and Drysdale won the war and they won it not so much by their agent's maneuvering as by the fact that the Dodgers were hurting all spring. In one exhibition game left-handers Bob Veale and Luke Walker, of the Pittsburgh

Pirates, combined to pitch a 5-0 no-hit-no-run game against them.

"They're five weeks behind the other pitchers in training," said Manager Walter Alston, when the holdout was over. "The thing we'll all worry about now is to keep them from hurting their arms."